God's Listeners

For Connie Foss-d
Enjoy!
John Saye

God's Listeners

AN ANTHOLOGY

John Sager

ISBN: 1519327684
ISBN 13: 9781519327680

Also by John Sager

A Tiffany Monday — An Unusual Love Story, WestBow Press, 2012

Joan's Gallery, 50 Years of Artistry by Joan Kohl Johnson Sager, Blurb, Inc. 2013

Uncovered — My Half-Century with the CIA, WestBow Press, 2013

Night Flight A Novel, Create Space, 2013

Operation Nighthawk A Novel, Create Space, 2014

Moscow at Midnight A Novel, Create Space, 2014

The Jihadists' Revenge A Novel, Create Space, 2014

Mole A Novel, Create Space 2015

Capital Crises A Novel, Create Space 2015

Dedication

To the chaplains who serve each of the twelve CRC campuses. You are the men and women to whom we BeFrienders turn as we seek godly wisdom.

A BeFriender's Calling

§

The invitation to BeFriend
is given as the Lord descends
through sacred flame to willing hearts
creating holy ground.

God's presence grants us sacred space
in which we offer God's embrace
by listening with open hearts
without the need to judge.

BeFriending is a call to care
most anytime or anywhere
as we become the arms of God
upholding hurting hearts.

Greg Asimakoupoulos
Chaplain
Covenant Shores
Mercer Island, WA

Acknowledgements

ANY AUTHOR SHOULD RECOGNIZE THOSE who have contributed to his final product. As it happens, I am one of several members of the BeFriender team at Covenant Shores, Mercer Island, Washington. Without their help, this project could not have happened. I want to thank, especially, Mary Nehring. Mary and I were the first BeFrienders to be trained for this mission at Covenant Shores, in January 2012, and since then she has been our team's most steadying influence. She agreed to read and re-read each chapter of this book and her suggestions and, yes, criticisms, have been especially helpful.

And I should mention my beautiful stepdaughter, Janice Bornstein. A lovely Christian woman, it was Janice who some time ago urged me to take on a project like this, something related to my 'faith story,' rather than another novel. Thank you, Janice!

And last, but certainly not least, I must acknowledge Barbara Schwery, the Executive Director of BeFriender ministry. It was Barb who, after reading the first chapter of the early manuscript, encouraged me to complete the project. Since then she has read every word and has offered a number of helpful suggestions. As one might expect, her ideas have made the work a much better product.

Preface

§

THIS GROUP OF TEN SHORT stories is about BeFriender Ministry – A Listening Presence. Today, some thirty-four years after its inception, the ministry is in place on each campus of the Covenant Retirement Communities organization. There are twelve of these, reaching from Covenant Village in Cromwell, Connecticut to Covenant Shores on Mercer Island, Washington and Mt. Miguel Covenant Village near San Diego. As the names suggest, each campus enjoys the support and blessings of the Evangelical Covenant Church of America.

BeFrienders listen to people of every faith, even when the person might feel challenged or doubt his or her faith. BeFrienders also visit people who say they do not have a faith, or believe in God.

To learn more about BeFriender Ministry and its guiding principles, please visit www.befrienderministry.org.

Readers who are not familiar with the organization of a typical CRC campus should understand that there usually are at least three levels of care:

1. Independent Living. Apartments of various sizes. Residents are free to come and go as though they were living in any other community. They may or may not take their meals in the campus dining facility and each apartment provides a fully-equipped kitchen, as well as bedroom(s), living room, dining area, den, etc.

2. Assisted Living. Smaller apartments for singles or couples, with meals provided in a common dining room.
3. On most campuses, a separate, smaller unit to care for residents who are dealing with memory loss, with specially-trained professional care-givers on duty, 24/7.
4. Health Center. A skilled nursing facility, staffed by professional nurses and others.

§

So, why a fictional account of an up-and-running and very real organization?

Each chapter is a stand-alone story and I intend to use fictional situations as a lens through which to view real-life circumstances and real people, drawn from my own experiences—and those of other BeFrienders.

One of the guiding principles of the BeFrienders ministry is this: to *care*, not to *cure*. Years of experience have shown that most people, when given opportunity to share their worries and concerns—with a sympathetic and caring listener—find it within themselves to discover their own cures.

It is true that nearly every BeFriender experiences, eventually, an intimate and quite personal relationship with the person he/she is befriending. These relationships are rooted in trust and that trust relies on absolute confidentiality. The person befriended knows, without doubt, that what he/she shares goes no further. Of course, God knows, but no one else.

Thus the title, *God's Listeners.*

John Sager
Mercer Island, Washington
Fall, 2015

BeFriender Ministry
logo

BeFriender
MINISTRY

A Listening Presence

The BeFriender Ministry Logo

Used with permission from BeFriender Ministry—A Listening Presence
1120 E. 80th Street, Suite 105
Bloomington, MN55420

1. The Words: As we look at the picture, we see the words that remind us that this is the ministry of being a friend. It is not about counseling or performing tasks. It is the ministry of being a listener, a companion on a journey. It does not take the place of family or friends. It provides a different kind of safe listening place. It comes into being for a specific purpose and for a limited time.

2. The Waves: The symbol of life-giving water suggests refreshment, cleansing and healing. From the Gospels we learn that after his baptism in the Jordan River, Jesus went forth in public ministry to proclaim the saving power of God and to offer a healing, compassionate presence. All baptized Christians are called to ministry.

3. The Hands: The image of the hands is in a mutual, sturdy grasp, suggesting trust and support. The connection is firm, yet gentle, allowing freedom of choice for both the BeFriender and the one being visited.

4. The Shafts of Wheat: Wheat is a sign of nourishment and the Eucharist or Holy Communion. It is also a part of the Gospel story of the loaves and fishes. This story encourages us by letting

us know that though the need is great, with God's help, there is enough. BeFrienders and those they visit often experience a communion in the sharing of the story. The wheat shafts are touching both hands because in this mutual relationship, both are nourished. They also experience a deep connection with one another and with God.

5. The Church Window: The picture is in the shape of a church window. BeFriender Ministry is a way of being church with and for one another.

Table of Contents

CHAPTER 1

Sam

§

SITTING ON A TALL STOOL in his church's brightly-lit atrium, Samuel Mandelbaum had to wonder how many of his friends had come to her memorial service. Most of these people he knew, those he didn't—probably their names would appear in the book that everyone signs as they enter the sanctuary. That way he could acknowledge their presence: so many thank-you notes to write, but she would have wanted it that way.

Sam's right hand actually hurt by the time the last of them left; so many well-wishers, each one with a kind word or two. And how would he survive without her? It was a question he'd asked himself while composing her obituary for the local newspaper. Then there was the service itself to organize. He left most of that to their Lutheran pastor, a sixty-something godly woman who had seen it all. She'd told her congregation several weeks earlier that she was about to retire but that was just a few days before his wife died. Now, with Hilda gone, Sam thought he should talk to the woman very soon. She had known Sam and Hilda ever since he joined her church; how many years ago was that? Too many to count, for sure, but pastor Sarah would listen to Sam and give him some ideas about what to do next. She'd seen many widowers come and go and Sam knew that Sarah Lindquist would have time for a nice, long chat.

§

It was the loneliest evening of his life, having to fix supper without Hilda. She had been a very good cook and Sam had learned quickly. Sometimes they'd have a 'cook-off,' to see which one could turn out the best evening meal. For tonight, though, it was a frozen pizza, piping hot out of the microwave, along with a glass of Merlot and a small green salad; then off to bed. Maybe he'd feel better in the morning but he doubted it.

Sleep came hard for Sam, the first night in some sixty years that he knew he'd be sleeping alone for as many more years as God gave him. He had nothing to do the next day, so it didn't matter if he slept. And so he just lay there, eyes open, staring at the darkened ceiling, recounting his past. In his mind's eye, he'd re-played the scenes many times, even sharing them with Hilda a time or two.

§

Immediately following the Japanese attack on Pearl Harbor, Sam enlisted in the US Navy. As an ace student in the University of Washington's engineering department, and with a 3.6 GPA to prove it, Sam told the recruiter he wanted to learn to fly and he thought the Navy should be willing to teach him. The recruiter told him that it wasn't that simple: He'd have to take an aptitude test, just like everyone else, and that would determine if the Navy considered him suitable for its rigorous training program. The aptitude test was a breeze and within six months he finished flight school at the US Navy's training facility at Pensacola, Florida. Following the commissioning ceremony, Sam was now a Lieutenant JG, qualified to fly two airplanes, the Grumman F-4-F *Hellcat* fighter plane and a torpedo bomber, also built by Grumman, the TBF *Avenger*.

His training at Pensacola had included simulated carrier landings, landing on a hard-surfaced runway that had been configured to represent the flight deck of an aircraft carrier. And it wasn't long before Sam was doing the real thing, in the far Western Pacific Ocean, flying off the deck of the USS *Independence*. Most of his patrols were at night as his squadron of F-4-Fs tested the Japanese air defense systems, flying as close to the Japanese home islands as they dared. The idea was to learn how quickly the Japs would respond by sending up a bunch of their Zero fighters, then one of the best airplanes in the skies. Thinking back on it, Sam had to admit they were all lucky. He never saw a Zero; probably just as well.

Flying the Avenger was something entirely different. Over the course of the war, Sam's torpedo bomber—he'd named it *The Gallant Lady*—had sunk, or badly damaged, six Japanese warships; two destroyers, one heavy cruiser, and three supply ships. When he mustered out, a month after the war ended in 1945, Sam was awarded the Distinguished Flying Cross. It was the Chief of Naval Operations himself, at an awards ceremony at the Pentagon, who pinned the medal on Sam, one of his proudest moments.

It didn't take long for Sam to get back into civilian life. He returned to the Seattle area, enrolled at the University of Washington, this time as a graduate student, and began studying everything he could find that had to do with airplanes. He'd heard that the nearby Boeing Airplane Company was hiring qualified engineers as fast as it could find them. The company had just finished the roll-out of its last B-29 bomber and was gearing up for peacetime production. Sam believed he could become part of that and after talking to the head of the engineering department he enrolled in a two-year program that would focus on structural design and materials analysis.

As with all returning veterans, Sam's education was being paid for by the US Government's GI Bill. With the money he'd saved during the war, he had enough to join one of the many fraternities near the university's campus. He soon discovered, however, that only one of these was gladly accepting of Jews, Zeta Beta Tau. That bothered Sam. In his military life he had never been aware of any kind of discrimination. If you were willing to risk your life for your country, that was all that mattered.

During rush week that Fall, the ZBTs saw in Sam something of an anomaly. He was at least three years older than the other guys, most of whom were fresh out of high school. And, too, Sam was already enrolled in a graduate degree program. But he should be a strong leader and a good influence on the younger men and so the house president offered Sam immediate entry into the brotherhood. That meant that Sam avoided the 'process' known as Hell Week, something he probably would have refused to endure.

As he lay there, still hoping that sleep might come, Sam decided that that entry into the ZBT fraternity was the best thing that ever happened to him. He quickly discovered something called an 'exchange,' whereby at least once a month a sorority invited the members of a fraternity to visit, usually on a Friday evening after dinner. It was the university's way to encourage young men and women to meet and get to know each other.

Sam's first experience with an exchange took him and his fraternity brothers to the Alpha Phi sorority house, just a short walk from the ZBT house. Sam was expecting a few questioning stares from the young women, he being obviously older than the others and even, perhaps, better looking. What he was *not* expecting was the sight of this beautiful, blonde woman, probably no more than eighteen years old, sitting by herself on a small couch in the Alpha Phi library. Sam was thinking to himself *I saw her first* and he hurried over, introduced himself and sat down beside her.

Hilda Jansen was her name and she had graduated a few months earlier from Seattle's Roosevelt high school. Without bragging about it, she told

Sam that she had been the school's May Day Queen, editor of the school's newspaper and its drill team leader. She had been one of the school's commencement speakers and, with a 3.45 GPA, her application for admission to the university was, as she put it, 'a no brainer.'

As it was still early in the Fall semester, Sam wondered if this blonde, blue-eyed beauty already had a boy friend, or maybe more than one, on the U-Dub campus. And what about left-overs from Roosevelt? Sam soon discovered that she was easy to talk to. She told him she'd never gone steady while in high school, that she was a committed Christian who planned on waiting until the right man came along. She had lots of time and intended to enjoy her studies at the university's school of fine arts. She'd been experimenting with water colors for some time and believed she had enough talent to some day do a show or two of her own.

And what were Sam's plans?, she wanted to know. Sam told her he was in a two-year program in the school's engineering department and that he hoped to land a job with the Boeing company as soon as he finished. But, he asked, what has *Christianity* to do with anything? I happen to be Jewish and right now I'm going to Saturday services at the De Hirsch Sinai synagogue in downtown Seattle. But after what I saw during the war I have to wonder how a loving God could allow such pain and suffering. In fact, I told rabbi Levin just last week that I was thinking about giving up on religion, just chuck the whole thing.

Not only was Hilda easy to talk to but she could be brutally frank, at the same time friendly and understanding. She told Sam that Christians didn't look at it that way. They recognize the evil in the world—what else could account for the war??—but that God has a plan for each one of us, if we'll just trust Him to show us the way. She understood that Jews don't accept Jesus as their Messiah but that's not to say that Jews and Christians can't get along with each other. Her advice for Sam: Don't give up on your Jewish faith. God loves each and every one of us, whether we believe or don't believe.

§

As Sam lay there, recounting that first meeting with the young woman who would become his wife, he still marveled at her maturity. This was an eighteen-year-old girl, fresh out of high school and, although she didn't need to say it, she seemed to have all the confidence in the world: a future without limits. Could that, he wondered, have something to do with her *faith*? And that question had led to another as he sat beside her that evening in the sorority house: Would she be willing to go out with him, his and perhaps hers, too, first date as new students at the University of Washington?

Much to his surprise and delight, Hilda said 'Yes.' He couldn't remember what they did on that first date. At the time, neither of them had an automobile, probably they walked down to the Ave and saw a movie, followed by a Coke and French Fries at the nearby McDonalds. He did remember that when he walked her back to the Alpha Phi house, she let him kiss her goodnight. And that goodnight kiss was the first of many. The two of them almost instantly had become an item, love at first sight.

Within a few weeks everyone in the two houses understood that Sam and Hilda were a 'pair,' and likely to remain such until they married. One evening in late May, Sam proposed marriage to this girl of his dreams; her response was something he never could have anticipated.

"Sam, of course I love you and of course I want to be your wife. How does it go, 'For as long as we both shall live?' But—and we've talked about this before—you still haven't figured out who Jesus is and until you do that, I can't say 'Yes,' even though I'd like nothing better.

"Sam, I've heard about too many young Christian women who think they'll be able to change their husbands after they marry; but that hardly ever happens and the marriage rocks along until one or both of them decide to call it quits. That's the last thing I want to happen. *Please*, Sam."

§

As he thought about it, Sam had to admit that Hilda's rebuff probably changed his life. At her suggestion he had talked to his rabbi and explained his predicament. Either he learned about Jesus and accepted Him as his Lord and Savior or he and Hilda would never marry. And that meant giving up his Jewish faith—what was left of it—and becoming a Christian.

Sam's rabbi saw that he had little choice and he reluctantly agreed that Sam could do what he thought necessary. And so Sam turned away from Judaism and joined Hilda's Evangelical Lutheran Church. He wanted to 'figure out' just who is this Person? Hilda had been a member since she was in grade school and she knew virtually everyone in the congregation. There were two older men who had been members for at least twenty years, both of them deacons and one a past-president. If anyone could help Sam learn about Jesus, these two certainly could.

§

If he was nothing else, Sam was a quick learner. He later calculated that during that two-month period he and his two new Lutheran friends had consumed at least five gallons of black coffee, sitting in the church library and talking about Jesus. The library shelves held a half-dozen books on the subject of Christian *apologetics*, a word alien to Sam. Fred Seaton, the past-president, put it this way. "Sam, the word comes from the Greek, *apologia*. In English it's the same thing as a 'defense,' or in the legal sense an 'explanation,' something that a lawyer would use to present his case to a jury, to convince them that they should believe what his witnesses had said. That's what these books are about. They explain the simple truths of the Christian faith. They present the evidence that Jesus really walked on this earth, that He and His disciples were hated by the Jewish leaders of His day and that that hatred led to His crucifixion as a common criminal on Calvary's cross. It's all there, Sam, and you can be absolutely certain of it. Look around you: There are at least three hundred people in this congregation who believe what we believe. Is it likely that each of us is *wrong*?

"And another thing, Sam. We Christians believe that whenever we have doubts, we go to the Lord in prayer and we ask Him. We ask Him to tell us where the truth lies. And you can do the same thing, Sam. Try it; you won't be disappointed."

He could recall that moment almost as if it had happened yesterday. It was the most important turning point of his life because now he and Hilda Jansen could plan their future, secure in the knowledge that they would, indeed, be together 'until death do us part.'

Sam remembered devoting the next two months to asking questions of anyone who would listen to him, virtually everyone in Hilda's church, men, women, even a few teenagers. Who is/was Jesus? Can I trust the Bible stories? Who was the Apostle Paul? What about Peter and John and the others? And did He *really* die on that cross? Did the Pharisees bribe the guards to say that Jesus' disciples stole His body? What about His resurrection? Is that believable?

By now, Sam and Hilda had made it a habit to meet in the library of her sorority house, the very same place where they had first met. They did this at least once a week, usually on a Thursday or Friday evening, knowing they'd have the weekend to catch up on their studies. But they didn't talk about school, they talked about Sam's growing faith. Hilda had been in church on the Sunday that Sam answered the pastor's altar call, walked up to the communion railing, kneeled, prayed and then asked Jesus to come into his life. And when that happened Hilda Jansen knew it was time to accept Sam's marriage proposal.

§

As he lay there, still staring at the darkened ceiling, Sam recalled the next two years as the most exciting of his life, more so, even, than those thirty-five nighttime landings in his F4F Hellcat fighter, onto the deck of the USS *Independence*. This lovely young woman, Hilda Jansen, had become the most important thing in his life. And they had two whole years to explore the world that was waiting for them.

And explore they did. Hilda decided to compress her art classes into two years, so that she and Sam could graduate at the same time. Although they had little money, they drove Hilda's ancient Volkswagen Beetle all over the Pacific Northwest, well up into British Columbia, through the Idaho panhandle, all the way to Missoula, Montana and back to Seattle. They rode the Columbia River stern wheeler *River Queen* all the way to the Hells Canyon dam, then to Walla Walla to explore the lush vineyards of that region. Their next trip took them along Oregon's coastal highway, said to offer some of the most beautiful seascapes in the country.

And, finally, Sam and Hilda were married in her Lutheran church. It was a small, private ceremony; they'd sent out very few invitations. Sam's best man was one of his ZBT fraternity brothers. Hilda asked one of her Alpha Phi sorority sisters to be her bridesmaid. Before the wedding, they decided to rent a cabin at one of Washington's coastal resorts, this one at Ocean Shores. They still were church-mouse poor but decided they could honeymoon for at least three days. They wanted to be alone; alone so they could let the rest of the world go by and enjoy the intimacy that, up to that time, had been denied them.

§

Two o'clock in the morning and Sam was still wide awake. He crawled out of bed, threw on his bathrobe and slippers and padded into the kitchen; maybe some hot chocolate would help.

Still no sleep, but the memories continued to return.

Within a month of graduating with his advanced degree from the school's engineering department, Sam was hired by Boeing, just as he'd hoped. Hilda, now pregnant, got a job as a draftsman with a group of architects, its office located on the twentieth floor of the Smith Tower, the tallest building on the west coast.

Sam quickly established himself at the Boeing Company, where its design engineers were working on the first versions of the 707 passenger jet, an airplane that would soon revolutionize the commercial airline industry. He was assigned to the Quality Control Division, a position that gave him access to every part of the company's production process, making it possible for him to befriend most of the on-line supervisors, the men who made the day-to-day decisions that would determine the company's success.

These men grew to know and like Sam, his good nature, sharp mind, and his excellent memory. He often shared his wartime experiences, comparing the performances of Japanese airplanes to those the American pilots flew. To those other engineers, he made a lot of sense and they were quick to notice his keen analytical mind.

During his second year at Boeing, Sam was assigned to its sales division. Upper-level managers had decided that would be the best place for him, a man who loved his work, his company and its products. And he was not afraid to travel, with our without his wife. His supervisors calculated that within a few years, Sam could be one of their best representatives in the company's overseas markets. Promotions followed and Sam was able to save enough money to buy a new home on Mercer Island, which would become one of the region's most affluent communities.

Following the birth of their third child, Sam and Hilda decided that would make a fine family; no need for more kids, although it would have been nice if one of them had been a girl. Three brothers, two years apart, should be just right. Sam opened a savings account for each of them, knowing that when they reached college age there would be no GI Bill to help.

Hilda had long since given up her job with the architects, preferring to be a stay-at-home mom. Occasionally she would accompany Sam on one of his overseas sales 'adventures,' as she thought of them. The Boeing company's overseas business was booming and Sam was one of the reasons. Demand for the 707 had tripled in the years since it first hit the market and Sam and Hilda found themselves in such places as Copenhagen, London, Paris and even far- off Wellington, New Zealand's capital.

Years later, the Kiwis were proving to be tough customers, insisting that Sam persuade them that his Boeing airplanes were better than those being produced in Europe by the Airbus Industries consortium. Sam told the Kiwis they had many models to choose from, as the original 707 had long since been retired. Today they could choose a 737, 747, 767 and the very latest, the 787 *Dreamliner*, in service for only one year.

The company paid Sam well for his work, a small percentage commission for each airplane he sold plus a six-figure salary. By the year 2012 he and Hilda had seen their thee sons graduate, one from Harvard and the other two from Stanford University. They had to admit that life in 'the fast lane' had been a lot of fun. But now it was time for Sam to retire, after one more trip to New Zealand. He wanted to close the deal on the Kiwi's first purchase of the 787 *Dreamliner.* Hilda wanted to make the trip with her husband, each of them knowing it would probably be their last. They spent three days at their favorite hotel in Wellington, *The Intercontinental,* Sam wrapped up his business and the two of them celebrated in the hotel's restaurant. The next morning, on their way to the airport, Hilda told Sam she wasn't feeling well, something was wrong but she couldn't describe it.

§

Now it was three o'clock in the morning and still no sleep for Sam. And he knew why as the memories of the following days were almost overwhelming. He'd run this through his mind many times and the image was always the same: Hilda in and out of the hospital, weekly visits to her oncologist, chemo and radiation, all too little, too late. And then she was gone. The cancer, a stage three carcinoma, had taken her life in less than two months. But, as those wonderful Hospice nurses had assured him, she didn't suffer. The pain control was adequate.

Sam downed a couple of sleeping tablets and went back to bed. In the morning he'd visit pastor Sarah Lindquist. She would know what to do and Sam was desperate for help.

§

The next morning, at eleven o'clock in the pastor's office, she reminded Sam that several years earlier, at her suggestion, Sam and Hilda had driven to a retirement community, located in Bellevue on the shores of Lake Washington. Sam had forgotten about that visit, or perhaps his grief had erased it from his mind, but, yes, he and Hilda *had* visited the community, Bellevue Covenant Village. Hilda told him it would a good idea to add their names to the waiting list, as a kind of insurance policy.

"Sam, you should phone ahead and ask for an appointment with their chaplain. I know the man quite well. He'll want to interview you and explain how the campus operates. Then you can visit their marketing people who will show you what's available in the way of apartments. The process usually takes several months, so the sooner you get started, the better."

And that is what happened. Sam visited chaplain Peer Davison, a man who had been with the Covenant Church for thirty-plus years, now serving his fourth year at Bellevue Covenant Village. Sam repeated his life's story, chaplain Peer all the while listening carefully, asking a question now and then. When he was finished the chaplain asked him "So, Sam, what can we do for you? You're obviously a man who is trying to cope with deep grief, and that's never an easy task. But I have an idea that might appeal to you. We have here at Covenant Village something we call the BeFrienders program. Actually, every one of our campuses has one of these programs. It's part of the Covenant Retirement Communities structure. As the chaplain, I oversee the program but it's the people themselves who make it work. Right now there are eight people on our team, each of them trained to be an attentive listener. That's what they do; they listen. They don't offer advice but by listening we've found that most people have it within themselves eventually to feel much better about whatever it is that's been bothering them. And another thing: Whatever you share with a BeFriender goes no further. Everything you say is a sacred trust; we have a word for this, it's *confidentiality*.

"What do you think, Sam? Would you like to give it a shot?"

"Absolutely. What's to lose? How do we get this ball rolling?"

"Good. There's a man on this campus, his name is Steven Atkins. He's about your age, early eighties. Like you, he's a widower. He came here about five years ago, after his wife died. He's been in the program for four years and is very good at what he does. You'll like him, Sam, I'm sure of it."

§

Downsizing out of his Mercer Island home was the toughest part of the transition. He and Hilda had done a lot of entertaining over the years and had accumulated a lot of 'stuff' that was no longer needed. Fortunately, one of Sam's sons lived in the area, he knew several successful real estate people and Sam was able to sell the home within two months of his visit with chaplain Peer. The move to his new apartment was easy enough, a small second bedroom would serve as his office/library.

Very soon, Sam and Steve Atkins began a kind of 'routine,' Steve coming to Sam's apartment once each week, staying for about an hour. Steve mostly listened, while at the same time he encouraged Sam to say as much as he wanted to about his past, his relationship with Hilda, how much he missed her, what he thought the future might bring. Eventually, Steve sensed that Sam had learned to live with his grief. It would never go away completely, the hurt was simply too deep. But as the two men prayed together, at the conclusion of each visit, Steve knew that Sam's healing had begun.

CHAPTER 2
Elaine

§

As THE CEREMONY BEGAN, AND with a name like Zech, Jimmy knew he'd be the last of the graduates to be handed his diploma. No matter, there were only thirty in his class and he'd be able to join his parents soon enough. He had thought long and hard about how he might re-pay his father. Dad had footed the entire bill: tuition for four years, the fraternity house monthly payments, his books, everything.

Two years earlier, his father had told him that all he expected of his son was at least a B-plus GPA and in his final two years as an upper class-man, strong scores on all his final exams in the university's school of journalism. Dad had said "Remember, Jimmy, your Covenant Church expects you to come out of this college experience with your interview-ing and writing skills even better than they were when you first enrolled. The church needs a good reporter and Pastor Arthur is counting on you. There are stories to be told and you're going to tell them."

§

Frank Zech, Jimmy's father, was a well-known businessman in Biloxi, with good connections throughout the region. He'd made a small fortune in real estate and had served five terms as one of his church's deacons and two terms as the church council president. Frank's real mission was to spread the word of Jesus Christ as far and wide as possible and he believed his son could help with that by becoming a first-class writer. And so within a month of his graduation from Biloxi University's School of Journalism, James Zech found himself behind his own desk in the reporters' bull pen at the city's major newspaper, the *Biloxi Times-Herald*.

Jimmy's boss, Larry Stafford, had been with the paper for thirty years. He was a tough and critical editor but he enjoyed the challenge of helping cub reporters learn their trade. Jimmy Zech would be treated no differently than anyone else, his father's reputation and influence notwithstanding. In their very first meeting, Stafford made it clear that Jimmy would be expected to do what every other greenhorn did: cover the police and fire incidents, learn the names of the principals and how to interview them. He expected Jimmy to write a least three pieces each week. He could work on his 'religious stuff' on his own time.

And that arrangement was just fine with Jimmy. Most of the people he wanted to interview would be members of his own congregation, folks he could call on after the evening meal or on weekends. And where to begin? Well, his dad had suggested he begin with the story of Elaine Huntington Everest. And why not? Elaine was the only woman in Mississippi's storied history to have won the Miss America pageant, way back in 1954. It was front-page news at the time but by now most readers had forgotten, or were too young to have known about it. And in her later years Elaine was one of Biloxi's most well-known personalities, a beautiful and talented woman, whose *real* story was known to only a few. It would be up Jimmy to find those folks and then persuade them to speak to him—on the record.

And how to tell the story? Jimmy decided he would do as much interviewing as needed, then write Elaine's story as a monograph to be published by his church. If his editor thought it was good enough, it might appear in the *Biloxi Times-Herald*.

After talking it over with his dad, Jimmy decided to try his first interview at the Biloxi Covenant Village. The village had been in place for about fifteen years and it was located near the shore of the Gulf of Mexico, with a beautiful view of the harbor, the fishing fleet and a public marina that was home to more than a hundred boats—sail boats, cruisers, and of course the shrimp boat fleet.

At Jimmy's request, his father had phoned ahead to arrange an appointment for Jimmy with the village's Executive Director, Jayson Montague. Montague had been in the Covenant Retirement Community's system for more than twenty years, and at Biloxi Covenant for the past five. His reputation had preceded him: kind, a devout Christian, a courtly southern gentlemen and one who made it a point to know the first name of every one of the 350 residents within the first month of his appointment.

Jimmy walked in to Montague's office at precisely ten o'clock. If he was nervous he didn't let it show. This would be his first *real* interview and he wanted to do it right.

"Have a seat, Jimmy. Your dad and I know each other pretty well and I assume you're—what do they say?—'a chip off the old block.' I think I know why you wanted to talk to me, but why don't you tell me, yourself."

"Thank you, Sir. I'm writing an article about Elaine Everest and I understand there are several people living here who knew her when she was a young woman. That should be a good place to begin."

"Ah, yes. Elaine Everest. Quite a lady, that one. Sure, there's a woman friend of Elaine's who lives in Building Seven, just a short walk from here. Her name is Madeline Storey and I'm sure she'd be glad to talk to you. Would you like me to call her?"

Jimmy's interview with Madeline Storey took up most of the morning. He recorded most of it with his smart phone and when the battery gave out he took notes. He judged Madeline to be in her mid-eighties but her memory seemed to be perfect. She was a friendly and charming widow who had known Elaine from early childhood. Later that same day, Jimmy began writing the story.

"Yes, I remember Elaine very well. We met in first grade. Even at age six she was the prettiest girl in class, and the smartest. While the rest of us were learning to read, she was designing skirts and blouses for her home-made paper dolls and reading the instructions for doing it.

"I remember spending some time with Elaine's parents and they told stories about her great grandfather. He was born in 1863, right in the middle of the Civil War. I believe the family lived in Alabama in those days, they moved to Mississippi later. But in Alabama, and after the war ended, the family returned to its large cotton plantation. By that time, of course, president Lincoln had freed the slaves but several of them chose to remain with Elaine's family. So, even when I knew her, the family had at least one servant.

"No, I wouldn't say that Elaine was spoiled. Like I say, she was a very smart girl and she could see that she was born into a situation that gave her some advantages that the rest of us didn't have. But her family's wealth wasn't important to her. By the time she was nine or ten she had discovered she had been blessed with a much better-than-average singing voice and so her parents began sending her to a voice teacher who also happened to give piano lessons. So Elaine grew up knowing how to sing and play the piano, at the same time. In fact, she would have some of us kids over to her home and entertain us. Not to show off, mind you, but just to have fun with her friends.

"Yes, I want to tell you about that. You're right, of course, Elaine *did* participate in the Miss America pageant, in 1954; she had just turned twenty-one. She had to travel all the way to New York City because the pageant was held on the stage of the Radio City Music Hall. My parents and I watched it on television which, in those days, was still in black and white. Those TV pictures didn't nearly do justice to Elaine's beauty, but we knew and so did the judges., In fact she placed first and it was her lovely soprano voice that made the difference. She sang one of Giuseppe Verdi's arias, *O Patria Mia* from his opera *Othello*. It brought the house down. And remember, too, that now Elaine is a beautiful young woman. She had long, wavy strawberry-blonde hair and a lovely figure. It was my opinion that the judges couldn't have chosen anyone else. And, yes, you're right about that, too. That was the first and only time that a woman from Mississippi has won the Miss America title.

"You asked me about Elaine's faith. I know that her parents never took her to church because they didn't go themselves. I went to Sunday school every Sunday but I could never persuade Elaine to come with me. I had the impression that she would have liked to come but that her parents didn't want her to associate with Christians. And after she won the Miss America title, she was obliged to spend a year traveling around the country, doing endorsements for various companies and in those circumstances I doubt she found time for church, even if she had wanted to.

"It's a sad ending to my story about Elaine, but a year after her Miss America experience, we seemed to lose our mutual attraction. By that time her name had become a household word and, of course, she got married about the same time. Oh, we exchanged birthday cards for awhile but, truth be told, we just parted ways. And I've always been sorry about that."

§

Before Jimmy said goodbye to Madeline Storey, he asked her if by chance she knew anyone else living at Biloxi Covenant who might have known

Elaine, say in Elaine's later years. That would be an important part of her life story. Yes, she did know someone, a friend who had recently moved to the Assisted Living part of the campus. Like Madeline, she was a widow but her health wasn't as good as it had been a few years ago. However, she believed that Betty McCoy would be able to add to Jimmy's understanding of Elaine's story.

§

Jimmy didn't know anything about Betty McCoy, only that her health might be a problem. He decided to check back with Biloxi Covenant's ED, Jayson Montague. To his surprise, Montague told him that the word was already getting around the campus that a reporter was asking questions about Elaine Everest. Montague told Jimmy that he had asked the Assisted Living activities director if she thought Betty McCoy would be comfortable doing an interview with a reporter from the *Biloxi Times-Herald*. Word came back that, yes, that would be just fine. Jimmy should come to Betty's room about nine-thirty the next morning, right after breakfast. The AL activities director would sit in on the interview; that's the way Betty wanted it.

§

Betty's stamina gave out after the first ninety minutes, but Jimmy's smart phone had recorded every word. Back at his desk, he drafted Betty's recollections of her friendship with Elaine Everest.

"Elaine and I are about the same age and I remember meeting her for the first time, about a year after her Miss America tour of the United States. She and I found ourselves at a party that Elaine's parents were hosting, welcoming their daughter back and, at the same time, introducing her fiancé, a man named Cecil Huntington. They had met when Elaine was in Los Angeles and it seemed to be love at first sight. At the time I wondered if Cecil was drawn to Elaine, knowing that her father had set up a trust fund for her which paid out about a million dollars a year. He owned most of Biloxi's shrimp boats and had plenty of money. But I decided, after meeting the man, that he really did love her. He was pretty well off himself and her wealth probably didn't make that much difference.

"Elaine and Cecil were married in Biloxi. It was a civil ceremony because neither of them were believers and with all that money they didn't need to have jobs. So right from the start it was to be a life of luxury, although to give them their due they both contributed heavily to the more deserving charities.

"Elaine never told me why, but they never had children. Perhaps she, or he, wasn't able or, more likely, they thought their life in the fast line wouldn't be good for raising kids. And 'fast lane' it was. For their honeymoon, they flew all the way to Australia, then came home on a cruise ship. Elaine told me about that. On the ship, every night after dinner, she and Cecil went to one of the lounges and she would sing the latest hit tunes, accompanying herself on the piano. She loved the attention, of course, but with her voice she'd quickly gather a crowd. To say she became popular would be an understatement. And, of course, Cecil just beamed, he was so proud of her.

"But it wasn't all fun and games for those two. When they returned to Biloxi they established their own charity. They bought a couple of run-down motels in the midst of the city's slums and converted them into day care centers. They hired the right kind of people to run them and their advertising made it clear that they wanted the poor, black kids to be first in line for admittance. I never knew for sure, of course, but at the time my guess was that Elaine and Cecil spent a least half of their trust-fund money on that charity. In fact, if I remember correctly, one of Biloxi's aldermen asked the city to re-name a street in her honor.

"And, of course, over the years Elaine and Cecil visited just about every place on the planet where it was safe to go. They never visited Communist China but as soon as the Soviet Union collapsed they were among the first tourists to visit Moscow and St. Petersburg. In fact, when the American ambassador learned that she was coming, he invited a large group of foreign diplomats to come to Spaso House[1] one evening, just to meet Elaine and Cecil. And, no surprise, Elaine found her way to the ball room's grand piano and sang the very same song she'd sung years earlier during her Miss America competition. The lyrics were in Italian, of course, and the Italian ambassador came over to congratulate her.

"But the story doesn't end on a high note. Not long after they returned from the Soviet Union, Cecil fell ill and within two weeks he was diagnosed as having a high-grade carcinoma in his liver. Of course, Elaine was frantic and spent most of her time with Cecil, going through the chemo treatments and the radiation. But nothing helped and two months later, the poor man died.

"For reasons I've never understood, someone was able to persuade Elaine to have Cecil's memorial service in a *church*. And, if I'm not mistaken, it was a Covenant Church pastor who officiated. What I do know, for certain, is that at that memorial service one of the ushers was a man named George Fischer. At the time he was a widower who lived right here, at Biloxi Covenant. George had read about Elaine—who hadn't, for that matter?—and he decided to make her his own private 'project.'

"The very first thing George did was to meet Elaine at the reception following the service. He introduced himself, told her how sorry he was, what a terrible thing to happen to such a fine gentleman, and, if Elaine didn't mind, he, George, would like to stay in touch, a phone call now and

---

1 Spaso House. An opulent mansion in downtown Moscow and the residence of every American ambassador since the establishment of diplomatic relations with the Soviet Union in 1933.

then, to assure himself that she was doing okay. He told her he'd lost his wife a few years earlier, had endured the grief process himself and he had some idea of what she was going through.

"Well, Elaine didn't think much of this chance encounter at the time but over the next few months George remained true to his word. He phoned her now and then, sent her 'I'm thinking of you' cards and, eventually, he invited her to have dinner with him. And not just *any* dinner. This would be dinner in the Biloxi Covenant Village dining room and she would be surrounded by a large group of senior citizen *Christians*. Could she do that?

"Elaine thought about it, but not for long. She accepted George's invitation, found her way to the Biloxi Covenant Village and they had dinner together. I'd be lying if I said there were no ooh's and aah's when George and Elaine walked into the dining room that evening. You must remember, it was the first time, ever, that a woman as well-known as Elaine Huntington Everest had come to Biloxi Covenant.

"I believe that at the time Elaine was living in her father's mansion, high up on the hill overlooking the Gulf. She and George had become an item by this time, seeing each other at least once a week, and she most likely was thinking about eventually marrying the man. But she had to wonder what it would be like to move in with George, probably no more than a two-bedroom apartment, a small kitchen and no servants. But, as she told me later, she had fallen in love with George and it wasn't much longer that he proposed marriage to her and, of course, she said Yes.

"And so George and Elaine were married, right here in our Fellowship Hall, with our chaplain presiding over the private ceremony. Many of us were curious to see how Elaine would make the adjustment and we knew it would not be easy for her. No servants, making breakfast for herself and George in their small kitchen, maybe or maybe not lunch and then dinner in the lodge's dining room. I believe it was difficult for Elaine, at first, because every time she walked into a room, any room but especially the dining room, heads would turn, just to look—*gawk* might be a better word—at this still-beautiful and famous personality.

"But then something happened and I think I know what it was. Within a month or so, Elaine's personality changed. I'm not a psychologist but I think Elaine was still hurting from Cecil's death. Her grief had turned into bitterness. She said as much herself one day by asking me a question: 'If there is a loving God up there—as you and your Christian friends seem to believe—then how come he allowed Cecil to die such a horrible, painful death? I just don't get it!'

"I have to admit it; I didn't have an answer for Elaine and rather than try to fake it, I didn't say anything. But from that moment on, she was a changed woman and, unfortunately, it showed. Just about everyone who knew her came to think of her as an insufferable snob, someone who considered herself better than the rest of us. And, of course, no one was more aware of this than her new husband, George. He was beside himself with worry."

§

That was as far as Betty could go. Jimmy realized what an emotional strain it had been for her to share the story, the story of a woman she dearly loved. So Jimmy decided his next interview had better be with Biloxi Covenant's chaplain, a man he hadn't yet met but whose reputation he'd known about for some time.

Martin Dixon, the chaplain for Biloxi Covenant Village, was approaching his sixtieth birthday. He loved his job but had to admit to himself that the pressures were beginning to take their toll. In the past year there had been twenty-five deaths on the campus, each of them in the campus Health Center and, of course, Chaplain Martin presided over each of the memorial services.

The up side of his job was his stewardship of the campus BeFriender program. He had gone through its training program five years earlier and now the team had grown to seven people, three men and four women. Dixon especially appreciated his monthly opportunities to lead the Making Meaning meetings. It was there that he and the team listened to the stories of other BeFrienders, each month one story about a relationship with someone on the campus who needed what they referred to as 'a listening and non-judgmental presence.' These important gatherings provided opportunity for the BeFrienders to learn and grow, while at the same time observing confidentiality. All identifying information was eliminated or changed.

That's what BeFrienders do; they listen, the don't give advice and they don't judge and, usually, the person befriended discovers within him or herself a God-given inner strength that leads to healing and recovery.

Dixon had seen that happen so many times that he thought of it as a God-sent miracle, people helping other people, people of faith who truly believed in God's presence whenever two or more were gathered together in His name.

When Chaplain Martin learned of Jimmy Zech's request for an interview, he invited the young reporter to come to his office. But prior to the interview he wanted Jimmy to read one of the brochures that would explain to Jimmy what the BeFriender ministry was all about: how it was organized, something about its history, its requirements for training, the role of the chaplain, among other things. The appointment was set for ten o'clock the following day.

What Jimmy heard from Chaplain Martin was something he hadn't expected, but as he thought about it, later, it made sense. Martin told him that as much as he might want to help him, the BeFriender program had a strong commitment to *confidentiality*. He understood that Jimmy was doing a story on Elaine Everest but, unfortunately, the chaplain could not even confirm that Elaine was of interest to the program. What Jimmy might do, he suggested, was to contact Elaine's husband. If he should be willing to talk to Jimmy about his wife, then that would be okay.

Would the chaplain be willing to broker an introduction?, Jimmy wanted to know. Yes, that would be the right thing to do.

An hour later, Jimmy and George Fischer met in the campus library. George told Jimmy that he was well aware of the BeFriender program and that he was quite willing to discuss his wife's participation in it. He did request, however, that anything Jimmy might publish would *not* reveal George as the source. After the two men agreed to this simple ground rule, George told his story.

"Jimmy, by the time I proposed marriage to Elaine, I knew that she might not be comfortable living here at Biloxi Covenant Village. At that time Elaine was not a believer and, worse, she had some misguided impressions about Christians. And Elaine knew that I knew but, bless her heart, she was willing to take a chance. The loss of her first husband had been a terrible blow for Elaine and although she was a well-known and generally-popular woman, she was carrying deep grief which she did her best to conceal. What she needed most at that time was love, a love that could help heal her wounds, and she saw in me a man who could provide that love.

"After we were married and Elaine moved to the Village, it was obvious enough that she was having a difficult time making new friends. I think it was her grief that turned to bitterness. She just couldn't relate to people and within a month or so people began to think of her as a snob, someone who thought she was 'better' than everyone else.

"Well, at about the same time, our chaplain—the man you visited earlier today—he came to the same conclusion, about Elaine's worsening reputation. He spoke to me about it, at first cautiously, and offered to help.

"He suggested that he arrange for Elaine to meet a friend of mine, Jennifer Lomax. Jennifer has been with the BeFriender program for some time and has been quite effective, owing to her years of experience. I had to be honest about it and I told Chaplain Martin that I didn't think that was the best way to go because Elaine—who in some ways is a very private person—would consider it an invasion of her privacy.

"So I asked Jennifer to join Elaine and me for dinner, after I told Elaine that I believed she and Jennifer would hit it off. It was no secret that Elaine hadn't made many friends and so she agreed. Well, as it turned out, the two ladies became fast friends. Sure, it took a few months but eventually Elaine was asking Jennifer questions about her faith, just who is this 'Jesus person?,' that sort of thing. Jennifer gave Elaine a couple of books to read, one of them by Josh McDowell, *Evidence That Demands a Verdict* the other one by Lee Strobel, *The Case for Christ*. Of course Elaine didn't realize it but these are two of the best books on Christian apologetics: easy to read and very persuasive.

"Well, that was two years ago and for the past year Elaine has been one of the most excited and exciting Christians you could imagine. She attends every worship service, serves on the Spiritual Life Committee and is just a joy to be around. And at least once a month she sings at one of the worship services and that is a real treat. Best of all, Elaine is now assured of her salvation. She knows, as do I, that when the time comes we'll be in heaven with Jesus.

"At the moment she's in our Health Center, some kind of 'bug,' but the doctor says she should be okay in a few more days.

"And, truth be told, I'm probably the happiest guy on this campus. When I married Elaine I wasn't sure how things would work out. But I trusted my Lord and we can see the results."

§

A month later, after re-writing the story to protect George Fischer as his source, Jimmy saw his 'Elaine Story' published as a monograph by his church; four hundred copies and counting. With that success behind him he asked his editor at the *Times-Herald* if he thought the story was good enough for the newspaper. Larry Stafford read the story, liked it and asked Jimmy if he thought there might be some follow-up items to add to the story.

And so Jimmy put in a call to Chaplain Martin, who had just returned from the Covenant Village Health Center.

"I'm very sorry, Jimmy, but you should be one of the first to know. I was holding her hand when it happened. Elaine died just an hour ago."

CHAPTER 3
Celeste

§

FELLOWSHIP HALL WAS PACKED; STANDING room only, and not much of that. Amy thought to herself that it was the most beautiful memorial service she'd ever attended, and she had been to a lot of them. Ten, a dozen, maybe more? Chaplain Mark's homily had been brief and to the point: As everyone knew, Celeste McGraw was now safely in Jesus' arms, all the worry and anguish forgotten, over, finished.

Amy decided to hold back and wait until the hall had emptied. She wanted a few words with the chaplain, in private, and this would be a good time; the man was so busy it was almost impossible to find him in his office.

"That was a beautiful service, Mark, thank you so much. I had the feeling that Celeste was watching and listening; she would have been *so* grateful."

"Thanks, Amy. Coming from you, that means a lot. And now that she's gone, you can go ahead with your story. Is that what you have in mind?"

"It is, indeed. I've already finished a rough outline and I should have the whole thing finished by week's end. You'll be the first to see it."

§

Unlike many of her 80-something contemporaries, Amy Carpenter was quite comfortable at her desktop computer. And she was a competent writer, as well, having edited the *Arapaho Village Voice* for the past two years. The Arapaho Covenant Village had been in place—about ten miles west of Phoenix—for the past eight years and Amy had been one of the first to move in, just a year after her husband died. And she knew everyone because she had made it a point to meet and greet each new arrival; and chaplain Mark Eagleton decided, almost immediately, that Amy should be one of the first BeFriender candidates to go through the training program.

By now, chaplain Mark's team had grown to five, two men and three women, with Amy part of the leadership team. When Celeste McGraw came to Arapaho Village it was immediately apparent—at least to chaplain Mark—that the woman was deeply troubled. She had been divorced only recently by her husband, and this after a turbulent marriage of 54 years, and there were some issues with her daughter that she had yet to talk about. Mark Eagleton decided that Celeste McGraw likely could be helped by one of his BeFriender team and Amy Carpenter would be a good match.

§

As Amy sat at her desktop computer's keyboard, she decided to begin at the very beginning. And why not? She knew Celeste's story almost as if it were her own, after meeting with the women over a period of two years, usually once each week. And, of course, over that two year period the two women had become close friends. Amy doubted that Celeste had held anything back. Now, she had the privilege of writing the story, a story with a beautiful—if unlikely—ending.

During her very first visit with Celeste, she told Amy some of her family's history. She was born in Mesa, Arizona in the summer of 1929, just a few months before the stock market crashed in October of that year.

The Great Depression soon followed and Celeste, as an only child, grew up watching her parents struggle to put food on the table. Her father was a young lawyer and not many people could afford lawyers, so she became familiar with hardship, up close and personal. When she was five, the family moved to Phoenix where her father had managed to join a three-man law firm. That small partnership helped considerably with the family's cash flow and, finally, Celeste's mother was able to by her daughter two new dresses, just in time for her entry into first grade.

Her grade school years passed uneventfully. Celeste's parents soon discovered that their daughter was a better-than-average student, also something of tom boy as she moved into her teens. She developed a fascination with the Arizona countryside and often spent weekends on desert hikes, camping out with friends, hunting jack rabbits and ground squirrels with an air rifle. On one such outing she was able to kill a small rattlesnake and brought it home to show the neighbors.

Celeste, as everyone else who lived in the Phoenix area, was well aware of the presence of nearby Luke Air Force Base, sited some 15 miles to the west of the city. During the years of World War II, the facility was home to the US Army Air Corps training command but soon after war's end, a new generation of military aircraft appeared, including the F-84 *Thunderjet* fighter, the first generation of jet aircraft to come on line. The ear-popping noise produced by these aircraft soon became known as *The Sound of Freedom* and most area residents took a certain amount of pride, knowing that America's first line of defense was just down the road.

Maybe it was the tom boy in Celeste, or her insatiable curiosity, but it wasn't long before she was begging her parents to allow her to take flying lessons. She was twenty-one years old, had just finished a four-year program at one of the city's junior colleges and had saved enough money along the way—baby sitting, odd jobs in her neighborhood, part time waitressing, and a brief secretarial gig at a neighborhood pet shop—that she could afford flying lessons, at least a few. She calculated that by applying to the local flying school for group lesson status, she could probably afford to get her private pilot's license. The school was using the two-seater Piper Cub J-3, the least expensive trainer on the market and the favorite of many flying schools.

Not included in her calculations was the fact that the Korean War had just begun, Luke Air Force Base was on high alert, and many pilots already in the Air Force were likely to be deployed to Korea. Those F-84 jet aircraft would soon be involved in deadly combat, young American airmen risking their lives.

And then, Amy recalled, Celeste met Air Force Lieutenant Pete McGraw. Pete had been assigned to Luke AFB and on his days off he visited the same flying school where Celeste was now working toward her private license. Pete had already logged several hundred hours in the F-84 and flying a Piper Cub was, for him, like going back to a bicycle with trainer wheels. Besides, he knew there were at least a few young women either working at the flying school, or taking lessons. And as Celeste had shared with Amy, Pete was one of those as-yet-unmarried Alpha Males, always on the lookout for a good-looking young woman. He was also a charmer and he somehow persuaded the flying school operator to let him fly one of the J-3s, just for fun, he said. And why not take one of your students along? I could show her a few things about flying, and it wouldn't cost her anything.

Well, Celeste could hardly believe her good fortune. The guy was handsome, built like an NFL wide receiver, he had a smile that gave her goose bumps and, as far as she knew, he was single. And of course, one very, *very* good pilot.

During her first flight with Pete, he was careful to take it easy; no point in causing this young beauty to become airsick. He asked her to do a few stalls, reminding her of the recovery process, then back up to two thousand feet above ground, a few side slips and then down to the standard landing approach: downwind, base, and final. Pete did the actual touchdown but he was impressed that Celeste was able to bring the J-3 to its proper position.

After the flight, they had beer and hamburgers at the school's small lunch counter and that was the simple beginning of a romance that quickly morphed into something much larger. Pete told Celeste that he could drive over to the school every Saturday. He wasn't due to ship out to Korea for another two months and they could fly together at least once a week. By that time—if Pete could persuade the school operator—Celeste would have her private pilot license. Then *she* would fly from the left seat with Pete on her right.

Well, as Celeste later recalled, it wasn't exactly a romance made in heaven—the J-3 rarely cruised above 8,000 feet—but it was pretty close. Pete proposed to her—one Saturday afternoon, while they were flying—and of course she said Yes. Then—smiling all the way down—she greased the Cub onto the runway, a perfect three-point landing.

§

Their wedding was rather quiet, neither of them wanted to spend a lot of money, so they chose a civil ceremony, with a local justice of the peace officiating. For their honeymoon, they motored to the Grand Canyon, not that far away. Neither of them had seen it before, even though Celeste had lived close by all of her life. It was a perfect honeymoon, three nights in a comfortable lodge not far from the South Rim, spectacular scenery, good food and wine and plenty of time for making love.

When they returned, Pete drove directly to Luke AFB, this time to one of the married officers' housing billets, something he'd arrange earlier. Knowing that his time was short—his orders had been changed and he would be leaving for Korea within the week—it was, for Celeste, a whirlwind introduction to life as the wife of an Air Force officer. Several large parties at the officers' club, where she met many of the men who flew in Pete's squadron, and their wives. The young wives joked that they soon would be 'warrior widows,' waiting for their husbands to come back from the required one-year tour. And, for the first time in her young life, Celeste realized that these other women, each about her age, were just as she was: anxious, probably frightened, not knowing what to expect. They did know there would be APO² mail service, letters moving—slowly— back and forth through the military's postal system. Telephone service was out of the question, and any effort to send mail directly to Korea, outside the APO system, was impossible.

And so it was a tearful goodbye as Pete's squadron boarded the C-130 Hercules troop transport. From Luke AFB, they would refuel at Pearl Harbor, then another refueling stop at the Navy's base at Midway Island and, finally, to the military airport at Seoul, Korea.

From there, no one knew what to expect. Silence had invaded Celeste's life, for far too long.

§

Within a month of Pete's departure, Celeste discovered *one* thing to expect: her first child. She was both ecstatic and frightened, frightened at the prospect of having her baby while Pete was still in Korea. Fortunately, her parents were living nearby and they would be an important source of comfort and help.

The next few months seem to drag along, Celeste and her friends—each one the wife of one of Pete's squadron buddies—chatting in the officers'

---

2 APO, Army Post Office. The US Army's mail service that handled mail for both the Army and the Air Force.

club lounge, oftentimes having to endure boring bridge games and endless speculation about what life would be like when the war finally ended.

Mercifully, this routine was interrupted about once a month when a huge bag of mail arrived at the base, nearly all of it from Korea. Each time, at least one of those letters was from Pete but the wartime censorship requirements limited what he could tell her about what he was actually *doing*. He hinted that he had been flying at least one combat mission each week and, obviously, he was still alive and well. The rest of his letters didn't tell her much, an occasional reference to his limited social life, all of it confined to the officers' club at the air base near Seoul.

Celeste wondered about that. Other wives were learning that downtown Seoul was crawling with American solders, sailors and airmen wandering the nighttime streets, often enough finding and paying for the readily-available Korean call girls. And then, four months into Pete's tour, one of Celeste's closest friends and the wife of another F-84 pilot in Pete's squadron, hinted that her husband and Pete had gone into Seoul, together, to 'have some fun,' as he had written. And just what did *that* mean?

Amy recalled that when Celeste told her this part of her story, she was in tears, nearly hysterical. She was pregnant and the last thing she needed was to learn that she was married to an untruthful and unfaithful husband.

Celeste's baby, a beautiful seven-pound girl, arrived without complications, while Celeste's parents were waiting down the hall from the delivery room. Celeste already had chosen a name, something she and Pete had written about. If it was a girl, they would name her Amelia, after Amelia Earhart, the most famous name in women's aviation. With that important decision behind her, Celeste moved in with her parents where she and her baby daughter would wait for Pete to return from Korea.

And return he did, one year and two weeks after he had boarded that C-130 troop transport at Luke Air Force Base. The mustering-out process took a week and Pete was now a civilian, out of work and needing a job.

If he was nothing else, Pete McGraw was a hustler, a man who moved quickly after deciding what he wanted to do. Even before leaving Korea, Pete and his airmen friends had learned that there was an ongoing mini-boom in the American civilian airline industry. Pete scanned the local newspapers and then drove to the Phoenix airport. He quickly located the airport manager, introduced himself and explained his circumstances. What about Continental Airlines? He had heard that the airline was considering an opening in Phoenix, perhaps enough space for three jetways and the required service counters. The manager told Pete he had heard correctly and suggested that Pete apply to the airline asap. Continental was looking for experienced pilots and there were a few slots still to be filled. Pete could expect a month of training, learning how to fly the Douglass DC-6, the company's new, four-engine propeller-driven aircraft. For a jet jockey like Pete, the transition should be an easy one.

It *was* easy, and within two months Pete had his job with Continental. He would be a captain in one of the first crews to be based in Phoenix, and an important part of the company's start-up operations in Arizona's state capital.

§

Now that the McGraw family had an assured income, it was time to find a permanent home. Celeste and Amelia needed some stability and Pete was determined to provide it.

The Sky Harbor Airport, oddly enough located nearly in the center of downtown Phoenix, was to be Pete's 'office.' For his family's home they chose a modest, three-bedroom rambler on the outskirts of Mesa, about a ten-minute drive to the airport. The home was not new, but it gave the young family just what they needed and, best of all, their mortgage was affordable.

Celeste's parents helped with moving day, a Saturday, and Monday morning Pete drove to his new job at the Continental office. The following Wednesday, he made his first trip in the DC-6, Phoenix to New York City with a layover in Chicago, then back to Phoenix via the same route. While he was gone, Celeste began to realize that this was a pattern to be repeated over and over, as far into the future as she could imagine. As she thought about it, she became concerned about Amelia. Would her daughter grow up barely knowing her father? And what about those flight attendants who flew with Pete? Young, attractive and most of them unmarried. If Pete was willing to cheat on his wife in Korea, it would be even easier now.

Celeste's mother had offered to baby-sit Amelia whenever Celeste needed that kind of help. With that assurance in mind, she decided to look for a job of her own. For one thing, the family really needed two cars and the extra income would help. And it occurred to her, why not try to get a part-time job at the Continental office at the Phoenix airport? If she could do that, the family would have enough money to hire live-in help for Amelia and—just as important—Celeste's presence in the Continental office would give her opportunity to befriend the flight attendants who were flying with Pete. *That* arrangement, if she could make it happen, would complicate any plans he might have to cheat on his wife.

As Amy wrote out this part of her story, she recalled Celeste's mood when she talked to her about *scheming* against her own husband. She felt ashamed, guilty and sad all at the same time. Pete had seemed like the perfect man for her in those very early days, but now her dream had been shattered. But for the sake of her daughter, she believed she had to make the marriage work, however difficult that might be.

Celeste got the job she wanted and stuck with it for the next five years. Pete's seniority grew with the years, as did his income. As long as she was in that Continental office, she never had any reason to believe that Pete was cheating. Still, she didn't like it but it seemed to be working. She and the Continental flight attendants—most of them—became good friends, something that was very obvious to Pete.

At home, when Pete was between trips, the family atmosphere was good. Amelia was growing up to become a lovely young woman. When she reached her sixteenth birthday, Pete—still an Air Force Reserve officer—arranged to reserve the Luke AFB officer's club lounge. Amelia was free to invite as many of her friends as she wished. This would be her 'coming-out-party,' something they knew about only by reading the *New York Times* society pages. Amelia's parents insisted that there would be no alcohol, an edict that Amelia didn't much like. And although Celeste didn't recognize it at the time, this was the first signal that Amelia, much like her father, had become a free-spirited and very-hard-to-control teen-ager.

The morning after the party, at the breakfast table, Amelia let her parents know what she thought of the 'no booze rule,' as she called it. Did that mean they didn't trust her? She had been embarrassed, nearly to tears, and she didn't like it. In two more years she'd be eighteen and old enough to drink whatever, wherever and whenever she wanted. And, by that time, she'd have high school behind her and she could do whatever she wanted to do, even move out and find a place to live by herself!

When she had finished her tirade, Amelia stormed out of the kitchen and went to her room, locking the door behind her.

Celeste and Pete had had their arguments before, some of them memorable. But nothing like this. What kind of daughter were they raising? Whose fault was it? Why couldn't Pete control her?

Finally, Pete exploded

"Look, Celeste, she's *your* daughter, too. And you spend a lot more time with her than I do. Maybe you'd like to handle Amelia by yourself. I can always take a hike, and don't you forget that!"

Pete's threat, 'to take a hike,' nearly came to pass. They talked about divorce but eventually agreed that they loved their daughter too much to do that to her. So they agreed to a 'quiet truce,' as Celeste later described it. It wouldn't be easy, but it was the right thing to do.

§

And those two years flew by all too quickly. Amelia finished high school, decided to wait a year before moving on to college, and found a small apartment about a mile from her parents' home. Dad and mom would pay the rent for the first year, then she'd be on her own.

Not surprisingly, Amelia soon became homesick, admitting to herself that her father's gene pool had endowed her with one of Dad's less attractive traits. She had become a headstrong young woman whose judgment, at times, wasn't very good. And that reality hit hard one morning when she realized that she had missed her monthly event by nearly a week. She was pregnant. She was sure of it.

Now what do I do? Answer: Go see Mom, tell her the truth, stop kidding yourself.

Fortunately for both of them, Pete was off on a trip. The two women endured a ten-minute crying jag, then put away the Kleenex and began to talk about the possibilities. First question from Mom: Does he love you? Do you love *him*? Enough to spend the rest of your life with him? And, does he know about this? No? I'm the only one? Okay, Sweetheart. It's simple. You can have the baby or you can have an abortion. And if you're not sure about *him*, the second choice is probably the best one, much as I hate to say that. And if you *do* decide to go for the abortion, we can do it so your father will never know. It will be our secret, period.

And that is what happened. Amelia would never be the same, nor would her mother. Guilt cannot play favorites; it's Satan's way of reminding people that he sometimes has the upper hand.

§

Pete returned from his trip the next day and it was all Celeste could do to pretend, convincingly, that nothing had changed. But inside she was seething, convinced that had it not been for Pete's poor example—she was certain that Amelia knew of her father's indiscretions—this never would have happened. And it wasn't long before Pete realized that something *was* different. He came to feel that his wife was only *tolerating* him. There was no longer any love in her heart, any hope that the marriage could be repaired.

And, as Amy recalled, this state of affairs limped along for more painful years. Celeste and Pete decided to use separate bedrooms. In the meantime, Amelia had met another young man, this time a man she could really love. They were married a few months later and moved to faraway Seattle, where Amelia's husband had landed a job with the rapidly-expanding Microsoft Corporation.

§

The divorce proceedings moved swiftly, each of them deciding not to contest anything. Pete willingly agreed to an alimony arrangement that would guarantee Celeste a reasonably-comfortable future. The fact that Amelia was writing once a week, deliriously happy and pregnant again, made the process much easier than it might have been.

Pete had good reason to be so agreeable: a fact he hadn't mentioned to his attorney, or to anyone else. For the past three months he had been flying with—and wooing—Bridgette Bowman, a new flight attendant, a Continental new-hire. She was a beautiful young woman, young enough to be his daughter, but that didn't matter. When Celeste moved out of their home, he'd ensure a descent interval and then Bridgette would move in. Perfect.

§

Amy moved away from her keyboard, poured herself another cup of coffee and tried to recall what had happened next. She remembered receiving a phone call from Celeste, telling her of the impending divorce. Her friend was trying to conceal her anxiety but it was clear enough that Celeste needed a friend, with a sympathetic ear, in a big way.

"Hey, Celeste, why don't you come over here to Arapaho Village? You know where it is, you've been here before. We'll have lunch in my apartment and then I can show you around our campus. You might even consider moving here; you could do a lot worse. Of course, you know that nearly all of us are Christians, but that's a good thing. We won't bite, I promise."

§

To Amy's delight, Celeste accepted her invitation. During their lunch together, Amy told her about Arapaho Village; she explained how one applies for the residential living program, the approximate fees for each type of apartment, the several committees that a resident can volunteer to serve, and the weekly worship services that are available to residents.

During their conversation, Celeste had asked Amy about the *Christian* dimension of life in the village. Must one be a Christian to live here? Or is the village open to anyone? And who's in charge? Do you bring in a minister each Sunday? How does that work?

As Amy responded to these questions, she learned that Celeste had considered trying to get her husband to go to church, when it became clear that the marriage would surely fail if something didn't change. But when she tried to talk about it with Pete, he wouldn't listen.

In response to her 'who's in charge?' question, Amy told Celeste about the village's chaplain, Mark Eagleton. Mark came to Arapaho Village eight years earlier. He had been lead pastor at the Portland Seaside Covenant church in Portland, Maine. He had never been to the southwestern part of the United States and he knew that Phoenix was about as far from Portland as one could travel. Plus, he reasoned, everything about the Phoenix area and the people who lived there likely would be somewhat different. The change would be good for him and, he hoped, for his new congregation.

And that hope had been fulfilled, many times over. Everyone who knew him loved him. The man was gentle, kind, loving, and—perhaps significant—he was himself a widower, having lost his wife some ten years earlier. And, many believed, he was the best preacher in the Phoenix area.

Amy went on to explain that Chaplain Mark was the leader of the campus BeFriender program and before Celeste could ask the obvious question, Amy went on to explain what the BeFriender ministry is all about. Amy, herself, had been on the campus BeFriender team almost from Day One. It was a ministry of Christian caring and, Amy thought, it would be a very good thing for Celeste to talk to Chaplain Mark about it. If she agreed, Amy would ask for an appointment.

§

Celeste's conversation with Chaplain Mark—as she later described it to Amy—was a long one. For one thing, she embarrassed herself by weeping, right in front of a man she'd met only five minutes earlier. She'd never before had to admit to anyone that she needed help; and how could visits with a BeFriender possibly make any difference? Chaplain Mark mostly just listened, while Celeste seemed to be searching for excuses. Finally, the chaplain told Celeste that he intended that Amy Carpenter, one of Celeste's closest friends, would be the one who would visit her.

And that made all the difference. Celeste put down a deposit and after three months her apartment was ready. Then she phoned a moving company and a week later she was adjusting to her new life in Building Nine, Apartment 4430, Sunset Drive, Arapaho, Arizona, 85108.

§

Amy never did understand what happened next. But, somehow, Pete had learned about Celeste's move. Apparently his affair with the flight attendant had soured—he had never married her—and now he was thinking that, just maybe, he should never have left Celeste. He tried to reach her by phone but Celeste's caller ID told her it was Pete. So she didn't answer, but she did listen to his voice message.

After thinking about what she should do, she wrote Pete a letter. Later, she shared a copy with Amy.

§

Pete, I know you telephoned earlier today but I really didn't want to talk. The hurts are still too deep. A lot has happened since we split and you need to know part of my story.

For one thing, I've become a Christian. That may surprise you, because for all those years we never even talked about church; and we certainly didn't do anything about it.

You know that I've been living in Arapaho Covenant Village for some time. I'm surrounded by beautiful people, Pete, every one of them a Christian and some have become close friends. I attend a worship service every Sunday and have some volunteer projects to work with.

I believe you know about Amy Carpenter. It was Amy who persuaded me to move here, probably the most important invitation I've ever received. And after hours of conversation with Amy and our chaplain, I've learned a lot of things about what it means to be a Christian. Where you're concerned, Pete, I've learned about forgiveness. *God forgives us, 'as we forgive others.' That's right out of The Lord's Prayer. And I* do *forgive you, Pete, please believe that.*

On a happier note, you should know that I've met a very nice man here at the Village. Actually, he's more than 'nice.' I've fallen in love with him and we plan to be married within the month. And Amy has agreed to be my bridesmaid. Sure, we're both in our late seventies, but as I've learned, where The Holy Spirit is involved, anything can happen.

Goodbye, Pete. I wish you well.

Celeste

CHAPTER 4

Frank

MARY BETH WALKED ACROSS HER small, second-bedroom office and sat
down at her computer's keyboard. She knew what she wanted to write and
it would be a long letter. But that's what her son had requested and she
promised him she'd do it. 'Just be patient,' she told him, 'this may take
awhile.'

A few weeks earlier, son Robert telephoned his mother and told her
that his five-year old twins, Mary Beth's only grandchildren, were worried about Grandpa Frank. He had been in the Health Center for a week
as the staff tried to deal with his Parkinson's Disease. The family soon
learned about it and because the disease, eventually is terminal, Robert
didn't want to tell his children. They had visited their grandfather in the
Health Center and it was apparent that he wasn't the same. That worried them and they had asked their father 'what's wrong with Grandpa?'
Robert had tried to assure them that it was 'nothing,' that Grandpa would
be okay in a little while. Of course, Robert knew better and that is why he
phoned his mother and offered his suggestion: 'You know, Mom, if Dad
doesn't survive this Parkinson's thing, as seems likely, it would be wonderful for the kids and the other relatives to know more about him. He's not
likely to do much talking any more, but you could *write* about everything
you remember; it would be a kind of biography of my father and your
husband. That would be a wonderful legacy, something the entire family
would enjoy reading. But, Mom, you must tell the *whole* story, including

the sorrows and scandals. We've not yet told the kids about that bad stuff, but when they're older they should know the truth. And it's up to you to tell it.'

§

She already had an idea about how the story should be told. Over the years, Frank had been very honest with her, telling her many things about his past that he could have kept to himself. She had kept a diary, too, and she could refer to that when her memory wasn't as sharp as she'd like it to be.

Next question: 'Who might want to read this?' On Frank's side of the family, there were two living brothers and a sister and each of them had children and grandchildren. On Mary Beth's side there was her sister, her two children and four grandchildren. All together, maybe as many as twenty, certainly more if she included all the cousins. So, depending on the length of the story, she might even have it self-published. That would make more sense than running off a bunch of copies at home.

Her first draft looked like this.

§

PART ONE: GRADE SCHOOL
Franklin Jefferson Barstow was born in Clearwater, Florida, on April 18, 1940. In grade school he was an above-average student and at age eleven he realized that some of his classmates were playing baseball on the weekends. He asked his parents about this and they told him there was a new program in Clearwater, something called Little League baseball.

Would Frank like to join his friends and learn more? Of course. So the following Saturday his parents drove Frank across town to the Little League practice field. They met the coach who suggested that Frank could begin by playing catch with some of the other boys. Next, the coach told them the team would have its first workout—as a team—the following Saturday.

During that workout the coach could see that Frank was about ten pounds heavier than the other kids. And his team needed a new catcher. Frank, with a bit of coaching, should be able learn that position. And with his size he might be able to bat fourth; the team needed a good clean-up hitter.

When the season was over, Frank had posted a .301 batting average and had been credited with twelve put-outs at home plate, an average of one each game, plus ten caught-stealing putouts at second base. And at the awards ceremony, Frank received a small trophy, acknowledging him as the league's best defensive player.

§

PART TWO: TEEN YEARS
By the time Frank was a senior in high school he had established a reputation as one of the best baseball players in all of Clearwater County. And he was a good student, as well. At the Clearwater High School graduation ceremony, Frank was privileged to make a speech as his class salutatorian; he'd missed being the valedictorian by only two-tenths of a grade point. Still, three years of high school and a 3.70 GPA was pretty good.

While still a senior in high school, Frank applied for admission to Clearwater Community College, already intending to declare a major in Business Administration. Frank had grown to love Clearwater's waterfront sights, sounds and smells and he had three friends who owned a forty-foot sailboat which was moored at one of the city's marinas. He anticipated that one of those marinas would be a good place to look for a job, even a part-time job, which would pay enough to help him with his college expenses.

On the day Frank visited the campus to enroll, he met a man who introduced himself as a scout for the local Class-A professional baseball team, the Clearwater Yachtsmen. The team was part of the Pittsburgh Pirate's farm system and its scouts were always looking for new prospects, young men who looked good enough to eventually succeed in the big leagues. The scout had heard about Frank's achievements and asked him if he'd be interested in trying out with the Yachtsmen. No promises, of course, but if he made the team they would pay him one hundred dollars a month, with increases through the season—if he was good enough. At the time the team had two catchers on its roster and Frank would compete with them for the starting job.

No surprise, Frank could hardly believe it. A chance to play baseball and get paid for it! Pittsburgh was a long way from Clearwater and Frank didn't know much about the Pirates although he did follow most of the National League teams. He'd never had a favorite but now that he was about to become part of the Pirates' farm system he'd better learn something about the parent team. Come to think of it, the great Roberto Clemente had been a Pirate, what, fifty-five years ago? Sure, and the Pirates beat the New York Yankees in the seven-game1960 World Series and Roberto had been elected to the National League's All-Star team.

Of course, Clemente had been the Pirates' center fielder and Frank was a catcher. And he knew he'd never achieve the stardom of a Clemente. Still, it was an exciting vision and Frank promised himself he'd do everything possible to one day become the Pittsburgh Pirates' best-ever man behind home plate.

PART THREE: TROUBLE
Frank began practicing with the Yachtsmen a week after his conversation with the scout. It was a tough grind, combining workouts at the practice

field with community college class work. But he stuck with it and within a few weeks his coach had him penciled in as the team's starting catcher.

After workouts, Frank and his new friends usually walked across the street to a small tavern. Beer and pretzels was the usual fare until one day some guy showed up who was selling marijuana joints, three for five dollars. That was when Frank learned that some of his teammates had been smoking the stuff for some time and he wondered how they could play baseball and smoke pot at the same time. 'No problem,' he was assured. 'Just be sure that coach doesn't find out. And never, ever, use the stuff until *after* practice.'

The Yachtsmen's season stretched into summer and by late-August the team found itself in second place, one game out of first with only two games left to play. If they won both of them, they would win their division and move on to the playoffs.

That afternoon, after everyone had left the locker room, two of Frank's teammates asked him to stick around for a few more minutes. Someone was about to arrive, a man who wanted to talk to Frank and his two friends.

What that man said to Frank, and his response, probably changed Frank's life forevermore. But, as I understood it, when Frank told me about it many years later, this is what happened.

The man—he identified himself only as 'Giggy'—appeared as though he might have been a nightclub bouncer; ugly, big, heavy, unshaven and he spoke with an accent right out of lower Manhattan. Without much fanfare, he told the three men that he was in charge of a local gambling syndicate, one that had been in place in Clearwater for some time. What most Class A ballplayers didn't realize was that there were heavy bets being made on the games. Some of this direction came from Las Vegas but most of it was local. And this gambling wasn't for chump change;

mega-dollars were at stake. And, as Giggy went on to explain, the up-coming game between the Yachtsmen and their opponents already had attracted about a half-million dollars, with more bets arriving every day. Most of that half-mil expected the Yachtsmen to lose the game and these three players could make that happen, especially Frank. The catcher, after all, was the team's captain; he called the pitches and directed everything else while the other team was at bat.

So, how to lose the game? Simple. The catcher—Frank—could make it happen and no one would know the difference. Botch a play at home plate, in which the runner is safe; allow a passed ball in a critical situation. Heck, only one or two runs would make all the difference.

And what if we don't go along with this,? Frank wanted to know.

Giggy's answer: 'You'd be stupid not to go along. If you lose the game you'll be fifty grand richer the next day. That's a promise. Think about what you can do with fifty thousand dollars.'

And what if somebody finds out about this scheme of yours,? Frank persisted.

Hey, man. We three are the only people who know.

And how do we trust you to make payment, after we've thrown the game?

Simple. The money will be on the top shelf of your locker; new, neat one hundred dollar bills, a stack of 500 of them.

Hmmm, that's easy enough for you to say, but I think we should get a down payment. You have any cash with you?

Of course. Never leave home without it. How about five hundred; each?

Frank looked at his two teammates, they were nodding in agreement.

Okay, 'Mr. Giggy,' or whatever your name is. It's a deal.

§

Well, of course Frank and his teammates were able to lose the game. But in the process they did make it exciting. The score was tied at four apiece in the bottom of the ninth inning. The Yachtsmen were in the field, Frank behind the plate, with runners at second and third and two out. The batter hit a hard ground ball to the shortstop who handled the ball cleanly and instead of throwing to first, as everyone expected, he fired a strike to Frank and the runner should have been out by at least two feet. And, of course, Frank deliberately dropped the ball as the runner slid across home plate. It was play he'd made many times before, but not this time. E-2 was what the scorer noted in his official record book. But Frank, and his two co-conspirators knew better. After the disappointed players had left the locker room, Frank and his two friends collected their money from Frank's locker and that was the end of that.

Or so they thought. Frank never did understand how it happened, but three days later an FBI agent appeared at his front door. He told Frank he had a warrant which allowed him to take Frank to the local FBI office for questioning. For the first time in his young life, Frank's *macho* was out the window. Rather than go to jail, he told the agent exactly what had happened.

The next day, Frank appeared in a small court room, with only the judge, Frank's court-appointed lawyer and the FBI agent present. After listening to the lawyer's explanation, the judge told Frank he would be on probation for the next six months, during which time he was expected to perform fifteen hours of community service each week. Up to now, the press was unaware of what happened and as far as the judge was concerned there was no reason to mention it. The game couldn't be replayed, nor could it be forfeited. The rules didn't allow that.

After leaving the court room, Frank asked the lawyer what he might expect from the man known only as 'Giggy.' The lawyer told him that was not for him to know, that 'steps are being taken' to run these guys out of town. They were smart enough to know that Frank had done his best; how the word had leaked, no one knew. But it was an unanswered question that would trouble Frank for many, many years.

As for Frank's two co-conspirators, they were tried before a different judge and he gave each of them six months in the Clearwater County jail. And, as I recall, Frank never heard another word from either of them.

PART FOUR: COLLEGE AND BEYOND

Frank finished his four years at the community college, graduating with a degree in Business Administration. He never understood why, but the money he received from Giggy seemed to have been forgotten. He kept it, all of it, and of course that made his college experience four of the happiest—and easiest—years of his life. During summer breaks he found work at one of the marinas, just as he had hoped to do and he also managed to continue playing for the Yachtsmen. Somehow, he thought, the baseball gods were smiling because that bobble at home plate was now ancient history.

It was in May that the Yachtsmen were playing at their home field in Clearwater. Frank couldn't remember what team they were playing, much less who won the game. He was still batting cleanup and as he stepped into the batter's box he noticed—some distance down the right field foul line and sitting on a chair near the bleachers wall—the new ball girl, recently hired by the club. Even from that distance he could see that she was one of the prettiest young women he'd ever laid eyes on. And she was good at her job. Several times she had snagged sharply-hit foul balls that were coming right at her. Frank remembered that at-bat went into the scorebook as a 'K,' one of the few times that season that Frank struck out, and on three consecutive pitches, so distracted he had been. As he walked back to the dugout he determined to meet this young woman. She probably would return to the clubhouse, along with everyone else, when the game was over.

And meet her, he did. Her name was Sarah Simpson, twenty-three years old. She called herself 'an army brat,' traveling to and from Europe with her parents, both of whom were serving in the U.S. Army as field intelligence specialists. She was an only child, probably spoiled—as she admitted to Frank—but she loved the game and had played women's softball while going to the American high school in Frankfurt, Germany. She applied for the ball girl job with the Yachtsmen as soon as she came back from Frankfurt and 'here I am.'

This time, Frank walked across the street to the tavern with Sarah. They had a couple of beers and French fries and talked until midnight. Frank told me later he thought it was love at first sight, at least that's how *he* remembered it. But from that day onward, after every game Frank and Sarah were together. Sometimes he drove her to her home and sometimes they just sat on a bench in front of the ball park, holding hands and talking about their future—together.

When the season ended in September that year, Frank and Sarah were married in, of all places, the Yachtsmen's club house. They had found a justice of the peace who was more than happy to marry these two, in a venue unlike any he'd ever experienced.

For their honeymoon, Frank contacted his three friends who owned that forty-foot sailboat. One of them could pilot the boat while Frank and Sarah learned something about sailing. At that time of year the Gulf's waters were calm enough and it would be something different. And there was enough room below deck for the newlyweds to have their own small stateroom, with another bunk-bed for the friend piloting the boat.

They sailed all the way south to Naples and then back to Clearwater, a trip of seven days. The weather was perfect and with the mainland never out of view they felt safe enough. But they were startled early one morning when Sarah spotted a school of dolphins, probably fifty yards behind the boat, moving through the water at what must have been 50 mph. They shot ahead of the sailboat and then she could see why: The were being pursued by three sandbar sharks, each about eight feet long but they would never catch the much-faster dolphins who were already out of sight.

After they returned to Clearwater, the newlyweds moved into a small apartment that was close enough to Frank's marina that he could walk to work. Sarah had brought to the marriage a Volkswagen Beetle and that would be their transportation until they'd saved enough money for something larger and more comfortable.

PART FIVE: TRAGEDY

When Frank first told me this story, he was in tears. Remember, this is a big, strong, macho sort of guy. But not this time, not when he told me about 'his' Sarah.

It happened right after the end of spring training, when the Yachtsmen were about to play their opening-day game at the Clearwater ball park.

Frank rode the team bus, expecting Sarah to follow, later, in the Beetle. But apparently Sarah was delayed getting away from home and she knew she had to hurry to get to her seat before the first pitch. It was a big deal at the time, because Frank, at the end of the previous season, had hit safely in each of the last two games, eight at-bats, eight hits. There had been a lot of hype about this in the sports pages: Could he continue his hot hitting streak, into the brand new season?

Well, Sarah never made it to the ball park. Some guy, driving a Ford 150 pickup truck, ran a red light and smashed into Sarah's Beetle, hitting the car squarely on the driver's side. Later, the doctors told Frank that she had died instantly, no pain no suffering. They also told Frank that the pick up truck's driver survived without a scratch and that he had been drinking, heavily. The police arrested him at the scene and would leave him in jail until Frank decided what, if anything, to do about it.

Of course, Frank was so shaken by all this that he asked the team's manager if he could take the next week off. He had to arrange for Sarah's funeral and then decide what to do about the guy who had killed his wife. Frank's manager was a sympathetic man and he knew his way around Clearwater, having lived there most of his life. As soon as the funeral was behind them, the manager recommended that he contact a lawyer, a woman he had known for many years, someone Frank could trust. Her name was Dorothy Andrews and she worked out of a small office in downtown Clearwater.

Well, it was a heartbroken Frank who walked into Dorothy Andrews' office. He told her that he wasn't interested in retribution. He'd driven drunk himself, more than once, but had never been caught. What did Ms Andrews recommend? Andrews had already checked to see if the driver's insurance policy would help and, yes, it would. All Frank had to do was go before a judge, tell his story, and he likely would be awarded the one hundred thousand dollars from the insurance company.

Now, at this point the story becomes quite personal. You see, I have known Dorothy Andrews since we were teenagers. We first met in a Sunday School class and have been good friends ever since. Dorothy told me about Frank's upcoming session in that court room and I decided to be there, just to see how my friend handled herself, and her client, in front of a real judge in a real court of law.

I asked Dorothy if she thought her client might be a Christian. She told me she doubted it very much, but beyond that she couldn't say much, the 'privileged lawyer-client relationship' thing. But she was willing to introduce me to Frank, as soon as the court proceedings finished. And that's how I met Frank. The three of us went to the courthouse lunch room, ordered coffee and donuts and chatted for most of an hour.

You have to remember that I was only twenty-eight years old at the time, still single, and already wondering if I might go through life as an old maid. Frank was about the same age and a handsome hunk, if I do say so. I think he probably found me to be attractive but he had just lost his precious Sarah and I certainly wasn't expecting sparks to fly or anything like that. But I did promise myself that I would stay in touch with Frank. Whether anything *romantic* ever came of it wasn't important; not then. I was hoping I could somehow lead him to know Jesus Christ. If I could do that, anything else was possible.

PART SIX: ROMANCE

I could probably write a whole book about the next eighteen months, because that's how long it was before Frank and I fell in love.

As one might imagine, Sarah's death left Frank in a deep depression. He asked the Yachtsmen's manager for a leave of absence, telling him he didn't believe he could maintain the level of play that the team and its fans expected of him. That request was a no-brainer for the manager and he told Frank to take as much time off as he needed. Frank's job at the marina was safe enough and he was able to work there five days a week. But the job had become boring, too much repetition, same old, same old. Frank remembered those young men on the team that were smoking pot and he decided he'd try that, too. Maybe it would help with the depression.

Well, that didn't work either, and so he decided to try something else, some of the 'hard stuff.' You can imagine that it wasn't long before Frank's boss told him he'd be fired if he didn't do something about his drug addiction. Frank, of course, didn't have a clue about how to shake his dependency so he turned to the Yellow Pages and found a clinic on the south side of Clearwater. And, as we all know by now, I had begun working, part-time, at that same clinic just three months earlier. So here, in the clinic, is the same Frank I had met in that court room, not that long ago. And, of course, he remembered me. The problem was that he was having withdrawal symptoms, sometimes they were severe, and all I could do was sit at his bedside and hold his hand, trying to assure him that he'd feel better in another hour or two. We did a lot of smiling at each other, never saying a whole lot, but I could sense that he knew I was trying my best to help him. And it probably happened that way. You know what I mean? Here is this super macho guy, someone who had never asked anyone for help, admitting to me that he had never before felt so helpless. He even cried a time or two, hoping I wouldn't notice.

It was another two months before Frank was well enough to leave the clinic and by that time I was seeing him every day, even though this was supposed to be a part-time job. When my supervisor asked me why I was coming to work every day, I had to admit to her that Frank and I had fallen in love and probably would be married by the end of the year. She asked me if Frank was aware that the clinic was supported by three local

Christian churches and I told her I doubted it had ever entered his mind to ask. But when it came time for Frank to check out of the clinic, he had to sign some paperwork. And right there, at the top of the invoice: *St. Luke's Clearwater Clinic.*

On our way home from the clinic, Frank asked me about that invoice: Who or what is 'St. Luke?' he wanted to know. And so I told him. He's the author of the third gospel and of the Book of Acts, nearly one-third of the New Testament. I'm not sure that Frank knew what I was talking about but that drive home was the beginning of a months-long Bible study. At first, Frank was a bit reluctant and, he admitted, somewhat embarrassed because he knew absolutely nothing about the Bible. But he also knew that as soon as we were married, he would become the husband of a committed Christian wife; and so, as he put it, 'I'd better get going.'

And he did just that. Even before our wedding, Frank began going to a Bible study that was led by the associate pastor of my church. He asked tons of questions, never wanting to 'buy a pig in a poke,' by which I think he meant he wanted to be *certain* that the things he was learning about Jesus and the Christian faith were truthful and reliable. Part of this transformation was helped along by two young men, about Frank's age, who had been Christians most of their lives. They answered Frank's questions, persuasively, and before long Frank accepted Jesus as his Lord and Savior.

PART SEVEN: MARRIED LIFE

As most of you know, Frank and I were married in Clearwater's Covenant Church. It was Wilson McKenzie who married us, the same pastor who was leading Frank's Bible study. We drove all the way to Key West for our honeymoon and after we returned Frank went to work at his new job. Frank used to joke that he might have had salt water in his blood stream, he was so attached to the waterfront and its many marinas. And, believe it or not, he went back to the same marina he had worked at before, only this time as its manager!

The parent company liked Frank's work and several promotions followed. He was making enough money that I didn't have to work; and a good thing, too, because I was pregnant with Robert.

As I recall, it was during that pregnancy that Frank told me something I'd known nothing about. I suppose he was feeling guilty, knowing that he was about to become a father and he didn't want any of his 'awful past' (his words, not mine) to remain hidden. It happened about a year before he met Sarah. Late one evening, after a day-night double-header, Frank and some of his teammates got together for beer and pretzels at that tavern across the street from the ball park. One of his teammates brought his wife and they were all sitting around a large, round table. Well, the wife happened to be sitting next to Frank and the next thing he knows, she's playing footsie with him underneath the table. This was an obvious come-on and within a week or two, she and Frank are seeing each other, unknown to her husband. And, sure, they slept together a few times, until she decided it was too risky. And Frank agreed, figuring the last thing he needed was a big fight with one of his teammates.

Well, I tell this story only because of the huge guilt trip it laid on Frank. He knew then that it was wrong and he confessed that it was still eating him up, ten years later. He told me that if he hadn't become a Christian, his affair with a married woman wouldn't have mattered. And even though, in his prayers, he'd asked God for forgiveness, it still wasn't enough. I tried to assure Frank that he certainly had *my* forgiveness. After all, this had happened before Frank and I had met.

If memory serves, it was about five years after Robert's birth that Frank switched jobs. But this time it was a significant promotion. Each of the Clearwater marina owners decided to ask Frank assume control of the marinas' logistics support. That meant that he was in charge of coordinating acquisition and delivery of all the supplies and equipment coming to the Clearwater waterfront. It was a huge responsibility and they increased his salary to the point where he would become a millionaire in another five years.

You might have thought—as I did—that all that success as a businessman would make it possible for Frank to set aside his troubling memories, to enjoy a life of relative ease and comfort. Well, you'd be wrong, as I was. Frank continued to brood over things in his past. One night, about two in the morning, he sat up in bed and in a loud voice said something like 'I should l never have kept that dirty money!' Of course that awakened me from a very sound sleep and I mumbled something like 'What are you talking about?'

Frank was so upset that he asked me put on my bathrobe and come out to the kitchen where 'we can talk.' And he talked for the next twenty minutes or so, telling me about how that awful man Giggy had crept back into his life. It was Giggy, you remember, who paid Frank fifty thousand dollars to make sure the Yachtsmen lost that baseball game. And—no one knows why—Frank was never asked to repay the money. He kept it, all of it, and after some time that made him feel like a thief, as though he had stolen the money. And if that weren't enough, Giggy somehow learned about Frank's new job as the Clearwater port logistics boss. And one day, out of the blue, Giggy shows up in Frank's office. He told Frank he'd be smart to place a bet on the upcoming game when the Yachtsmen would be playing at home. Only this time the fix was in with the opposing team, the Palm Beach Admirals. They would be paid to lose the game and anyone betting on that loss would make a small fortune because everyone expected the Yachtsmen to win; the odds were something like ten to one.

By the time Frank finished this sorry story, he had tears in his eyes. He said he felt as though the Mafia had his name on a short list of petty criminals. We finally went back to bed but neither of us got much sleep.

Then there was the time when Frank awoke about four in the morning, in a cold sweat. He'd had a nightmare, a kind of vision in which he saw Satan pointing at him and accusing him of being the cause of Sarah's death. If it hadn't been for Sarah's hurrying to get to her seat in time for the first pitch, the car crash wouldn't have happened and she'd be happily married to Frank. Satan's final sneer, before Frank awakened: 'It was your fault, Frank; don't you forget that.'

PART EIGHT: THE HERE AND NOW

I'm going to finish this story by bringing everyone up to date on what's been going on in our lives since we moved to our new home in Clearwater's Covenant Village by the Sea.

Not long after the doctor told us that Frank had Parkinson's Disease, we decided it was the best thing to do. A few of our Christian friends were already living here and they told us about the village's amenities, especially its Health Center. They also mentioned the village's chaplain, expecting that we would get to know him soon after moving here.

Of course, when Frank learned about his terminal illness he became even more depressed and, frankly, not much fun to live with. He had convinced himself that—because of the mistakes he had made along the way—he wasn't 'good enough' to go to Heaven. So, quite literally, he was anticipating an afterlife in which he would be forever separated from me and every other one of his Christian friends. Talk about doom and gloom!

I had been doing a lot of praying about all this and I believe it was God's plan that we would learn about another gentleman, Charlie Evans, who had moved to the village only a year earlier. And it was no coincidence that Charlie had played for the Clearwater Yachtsmen at the same time as Frank. He played second base. They were teammates and at that time good friends.

When we learned about Charlie's presence, right here on campus, it reminded me of the verses in St. Matthew's gospel where Jesus tells His disciples that 'with God all things are possible.' I truly believed it was a God-sent miracle, that somehow God had intended that Charlie and Frank would once again connect.

Well, this didn't happen all at once. After a month or so I visited the campus chaplain, a retired Covenant Church pastor and one of the nicest men I've known. After I told him about Frank's many concerns he began to explain to me how the BeFriender program works and it was then I learned that Charlie Evans was part of the campus BeFriender team. The chaplain asked me if Frank was aware of our conversation and I told him 'not yet.' Then he suggested that we meet again and that I bring Frank with me. That way, the three of us could talk about the BeFriender program and how it might help Frank deal with his concerns.

A few days later, we three had that conversation and when Frank learned that his old friend Charlie Evans was living in the same community it seemed to be the best news he'd heard in a very long time. Would Frank agree to meet with Charlie, Charlie the BeFriender? Of course he would, the sooner the better!

Like I say, this didn't happen all at once. Frank and Charlie got together at least once a week for more than a year and after one of those visits Frank came home, tears in his eyes, walked into our bedroom, dropped to his knees alongside our bed and asked God to forgive him for all the 'bad stuff' that had gone on in his life. And within another six months, Frank's speech had been so affected by his disease that he sometimes would 'talk' to Charlie by scribbling notes on three-by-five cards. It was all Charlie could do to maintain his composure as he watched his old friend slowly slipping away.

Charlie continues to see Frank, as painful as it is. Nobody knows how many more days God will give Frank on this earth but what we *do* know is that when the time comes Frank expects to spend eternity with Jesus.

CHAPTER 5
Gus

§

THIS STORY IS ABOUT A man whose life experiences may be the most unusual of any to come to the attention of the BeFriender ministry. It was written by the man's granddaughter and is reprinted here, with her permission.

My grandfather's name is Gustav Bjorsi or *Gus*, as he is known to his many friends. Gus is a senior citizen who lives in Bridgeport, Connecticut, in Bridgeport Covenant Village. The village was first opened by Covenant Retirement Communities in Fall, 2005, after the purchase of a hillside fifty-acre plot. Today, the campus offers a beautiful view of the Bridgeport harbor and about 400 senior citizens enjoy living there.

§

As the name suggests, Gus is of Norwegian stock. His grandparents came to these shores in the early 1900s. It was natural enough that they settled in the Bridgeport area, having come from a seafaring culture. Gus never knew his grandparents as they both had passed away before he was born.

And he never really knew his father, either. My great-grandfather, Lars Bjorsi died in a freakish accident while working in the local ship-yard. Gus was just four years old at the time. Alma Bjorsi, my great-grandmother, had never worked a day in her life but she now had a four-year-old son to support and after some searching she was able to line up jobs as a household cleaning woman. It was a tough go; sometimes she'd have to take Gus with her, other times she could find a friend to serve as a baby-sitter. But it left precious little time for Alma to be the mother that Gus—now fatherless—so desperately needed.

Things became somewhat easier for Alma when Gus was old enough to go to school. When he was six, she enrolled him in one of Bridgeport's elementary schools and she was able to arrange her work schedule so that she could be at home when the school bus dropped him off a block away.

Still, her income was barely enough to keep up the rent payments and put food on the table, and birthday and Christmas gifts were out of the question. Gus was a bright kid and he could see what was happening and so one day he asked his mother if she thought he was old enough to have a paper route. He had learned that one of his friends at school had one, so why not Gus? That way, he could help Mom with some of her expenses. It wouldn't be much, but every penny would help.

When Grandfather told me this story, many years later, he couldn't member how his mom was able to finagle the paper route, but she did and within a month or so Gus had thirty-five paying customers and a ten-year-old bicycle that his mother found in a pawn shop. Gus, at that age, had never heard of the word *entrepreneur*, but as he thought about it, that's exactly how he saw himself.

Unfortunately, as it turned out, Gus' inventiveness soon became potential trouble. Within two months on his paper route, it became apparent that every now and then one of his customers would tell him that they were about to go away on vacation, say for at least a week, sometimes two or three. Gus thought about this, always having in mind his mother's cash-flow problem, and decided he could help out. The problem was, how to break into the home of a vacationing customer without getting caught. His newspaper, the *Bridgeport Beacon*, was a morning paper and that meant that Gus had to be on his route no later than six o'clock in the morning. At that hour, he knew, his residential neighborhoods were relatively quiet, people still getting dressed, preparing breakfast, that sort of thing. And it was during those quiet times that Gus was able to find an unlocked window, sometimes even a back door that had been left unlocked. And when he knew that, it was a simple matter to slip out of his mother's apartment, say a little after midnight, go to the unprotected home and once inside, help himself to whatever cash or other valuables he could find.

Of course, he had to tell his mother what he was doing. How else to explain the extra cash that was now available? So, tell her he did, and—no surprise—she became very upset, nearly hysterical, in fact. But after she thought about it, she decided not to say anything to anyone. If her son wanted to be a petty thief, so be it. At least they'd have some extra money for the Christmas holidays.

Well, that was the turning point: Alma Bjorsi's decision to keep her dirty little secret between herself and her son. She knew it was wrong and within a few weeks the guilt had become more than she could handle. And with the now-available extra cash, it was a small step to alcohol and drugs. She used both in small quantities because she had to keep her job, but the dependency quickly caught up with her. And it wasn't long before she couldn't care less what her son was up to.

Some of the stolen money went for the purchase of a motor bike, something that Gus had been talking about because it would make it easier to deliver his newspapers. But Gus had become something of a penny-pincher and so he decided to steal the fuel that the motorbike required, low-octane gasoline. And again he chose one of his paper-route customers as his victim.

This customer and his wife owned a thirty-foot motor home, and kept it in the vacant lot next door. Gus estimated the motor home's fuel tank had at least an 80-gallon capacity. If he took only 20 gallons, the owner might not even notice.

There was a four-foot security fence surrounding the lot, secured by a locked gate. No problem for Gus. One moonless night, about two a.m., Gus hopped over the fence and siphoned off about twenty gallons of gasoline, decanting it into four five-gallon plastic jugs that he had brought with him. That was enough fuel to last a whole year; just another problem solved by Gus, the budding *entrepreneur.*

And then there was the time when Gus, on his paper route, spotted a man's wallet lying alongside the driveway of one of his customers. Gus gathered in the wallet, discovered it contained a hundred dollars in twenty-dollar bills. Gus pocketed the cash, and then mailed the wallet back to its owner; no return address on the package.

§

These are only a few of the highlights of Gus' young 'career.' There were others, of course, but my purpose here is to give readers an idea of my grandfather's initiative and imagination.

As I've suggested, Gus was no dummy and he should have gone on to college after graduating from high school. But he couldn't afford that and he had long since given up his paper route. Soon after his high school graduation ceremony—and he was number ten in academic achievement in a class of 250 graduates—he found a job at the local McDonald's restaurant. Like all employees of that chain, Gus started at the bottom, after learning how to operate the cash register and make change. (This was long before computers took over that chore.)

Well, it wasn't long before Gus figured out a way to scam the cash register. He did it by entering less-expensive meals than were actually served and, of course, he pocketed the difference. He told me that after a year at McDonalds he had more than doubled his income and his manager never did catch on.

Gus stayed with this job for three years and, believe it or not, management was so impressed with his work that they promoted him to assistant manager. In that position he no longer had to steal from the company and he began saving money and actually opened a savings account in the Bridgeport National Bank.

Then, one evening about eight o' clock, a very attractive young women came into the restaurant, someone Gus had never seen before. He decided he'd like to meet this young beauty and he told his servers that he would take the woman's order.

I should point out at this juncture that Gus was a rather good-looking man, probably six feet tall, a muscular 180 pounds and he had kept himself in good shape. He was also quite a charmer. He had deep blue eyes and thick, wavy blonde hair—what you'd expect of a Norwegian—and a quick smile. I'm sure that most women fond him attractive and of course he was single.

Well, this young woman was certainly flattered when Gus came over to take her order. His McDonalds name tag clearly identified him as the store's assistant manager. She ordered a Big Mac, French fries and a Coke, Gus all the time flashing that come-on smile as he scribbled down her order. Before leaving her booth he told her that—as she could see—she was the only customer in the store and would she mind if Gus sat with her while she ate. No, of course she wouldn't mind.

You can probably guess where this is going. The woman's name was Heidi Feldstad, she also of Norwegian stock, and Heidi and Gus hit it off immediately. In fact, I believe Gus told me she waited until midnight when the restaurant closed and then they drove together to her apartment where Gus spent the night. It was probably the first time in his life that Gus had actually fallen in love with a woman but after living with Heidi for only a month he felt certain that Heidi was his future.

However, Heidi didn't want to get married. She told Gus she didn't 'feel right' about it and so they decided to live together, for a while, to see if Heidi might change her mind. With this arrangement they were both able to keep their jobs—Gus at McDonalds, and Heidi just down the street where she worked as a waitress at Burger King. And Gus soon learned that Heidi had very expensive tastes. She told him she'd always wanted to wear a two-carat diamond and she was tired of driving her six-year old Ford Falcon. Could Gus do something about this?, she wanted to know.

As smart as Gus was, he should have known better. I suppose his infatuation with Heidi robbed him of his usual common sense, but he was determined to buy her that diamond ring and find her a more suitable automobile. So the two of them worked out a plan they were sure would work.

You have to remember that Gus was the assistant manager of that McDonalds restaurant. His boss trusted him completely and didn't mind taking a week off now and then, knowing that Gus would literally 'mind the store' while he was gone. And 'minding the store' meant that every Friday late afternoon, Gus or his boss would go to the back room, open the store's safe, and take the week's accumulated cash to the local bank. Gus had noticed that, on average, those cash deposits amounted to at least twenty-five thousand dollars, more than enough to buy Heidi her ring and to put a sizable down payment on a better car.

But neither of the two schemers wanted to let it appear that Gus had *stolen* the money from McDonalds. No, no. They had a better idea. Here's what happened.

About six o'clock one Friday evening, Gus comes staggering home to Hilda's apartment. He has a bruise over his left eye, his shirt is torn and one of his shoes is missing. He tells Hilda that on his way to the bank he was robbed by two young thugs who apparently knew he would be making the weekly deposit. He says 'Hurry, Hilda, call 911 right now!'

Ten minutes later, two police officers from the 23rd precinct arrive. They question Gus and Hilda, take a bunch of notes, especially while Gus describes the two men who robbed him. They ask Gus if he's willing to come to the station in a day or two. By then Gus could look over a lineup of local hoodlums, maybe one or two of the robbers would be among them.

Of course, Gus and Hilda never expected that Gus would have to go to the *police station*. Even if he did, the lineup wouldn't include the two robbers; they were make-believe characters, right out of Hilda's imagination. And in Hilda's bedroom closet was a shoebox stuffed with twenty four thousand dollars.

Two days later, Gus went to the precinct station, viewed the lineup and, of course, he had to tell the officers that his two assailants were not part of the group. More questions followed: Tell us more about what these two guys looked like, etc. And Gus probably got his stories mixed up because the police didn't believe him. They told him he could go home but don't leave town.

So Gus goes home and discovers that Hilda has moved out. The closets are empty, the shoebox is gone and she didn't even leave him a note.

§

I had to feel sorry for Grandpa, seeing his face tear up as he told me the rest of his 'Hilda Story,' as he called it. A week after Hilda disappeared,

Gus was arrested by the same officers. A judge asked him if he wanted a jury trial, which would cost the taxpayers a lot of money, or he could waive the trial and spend the next ninety days in jail and then go home.

Toward the end of the ninety days, one of those same arresting officers paid Gus a visit in his cell and told him what his investigation had learned.

It seems that Hilda had been a hooker who decided to find some honest work. She got a job at the Burger King and after a couple of weeks of chatting with her co-workers she learned about this man Gustav Bjorsi, who worked at the McDonalds, just down the street. He was the assistant manager and, like all assistant managers, he had easy access to all the cash that moved through the store. From that moment on, Gus had become Hilda's mark and Gus could finish the story himself. To make matters worse, the officer told Gus he was pretty sure that 'Hilda' was not the woman's real name. In any case, she was long gone, with the money, and it was anyone's guess if she was wearing a two-carat ring and driving a better car.

I want to fast forward now to a time when Gus is in his early forties. He's been in and out of prison several times but he was always a model prisoner and certainly never a violent man. He told me that after his demeaning experience with 'Hilda,' he became afraid of women, never trusting them and never, ever wanting to become romantically involved. His self-esteem had nearly left him and the only way he could support himself was by stealing. He decided, eventually, that he could let the state of Connecticut support him by 'living' in one of its prisons. And that is exactly what happened. Over the many years he spent in that prison system, he kept a notebook in which he recorded the things he wanted to be able to share with others, if and when he became a free man.

As I've said, my grandfather was a very likeable guy. He made friends easily, even among some of the toughest men you'd never want to meet. Most of their conversations, by necessity, were in the prison mess hall, over lunch or the evening meal. One of the first horror stories that Gus heard came from a man who was serving twenty-five years for second-degree manslaughter. He told of the time when his cell-mate was sexually assaulted while taking a shower. The man complained to the warden—who happened to be one of the meanest and most dishonest men in the system—who then accused him of lying and ordered the man put in solitary confinement for two long weeks. But, as Gus' notebook recorded it, prisoners have a way of communicating with the outside world. When the state's Bureau of Prisons had heard enough about this particular warden, he was relieved of his duties and is now trying to get by on a much-too-small pension.

Gus told me he's convinced that one of the problems with America's prison system is that those who choose to make a career of it aren't paid very much. It's the kind of work just about anyone can do and so there's no shortage of applicants. This truth was revealed to Gus when a new prisoner joined the others. In fact, he was assigned the cell right next to the one Gus was inhabiting, giving Gus an up-close-and-personal understanding of the man's problems. The man, it seemed to Gus, was certifiably insane and he said as much, as he tried to explain how he had come to this stage in his life. The prison doctor, himself barely qualified to serve, refused to consider any special treatment for the man who, after only a month in his cell, tried to kill himself by slashing his wrists with a broken drinking glass he had smuggled out of the mess hall.

But of all the stories Gus told me about his life in Connecticut's prison system, this one sticks in my mind. Gus wasn't a participant, but he learned of it from another prisoner who watched it happen. At a state prison—which shall remain unnamed—in western Connecticut, the prison's warden routinely organized outside work parties, groups of twenty-five to thirty men who were assigned to jobs for which the state would ordinarily have to pay union wages: truck drivers, power shovel operators, skilled carpenters, cement workers and others. But by using prison labor, these projects cost the state nothing at all. And the state made good use of this system, especially when if found it necessary to do repair work on its share of Interstate 84.

One of the warden's work parties was directed to replace twenty miles of obsolete guard railing on the Interstate and the contract specified that the job be completed before early December when the weather likely would interfere with the work. Over the years, the warden had developed some cozy relationships with a few bureaucrats in Hartford, the state capital, and he decided to call in a favor. He told one of his friends in Hartford that there was no way the project could be completed on time *unless* he added another thirty men to the project. That he could do but it would require a 'payment' of fifty thousand dollars, in the form of a cashier's check, mailed directly to the warden's home address.

Gus told me he understood this kind of bribery to be rare but, obviously, rewarding. In this instance the warden was able to double his annual salary with no more effort that a couple of phone calls. And now that I've thought about it, I believe Gus was implying that this story was just one example of many that somehow brought to him a deep sense of shame. He had chosen to 'live in the shadows' (his words, not mine) and what he saw there would haunt him for the rest of his life.

§

According to my notes, it was in 1976 or 1977 when Gus first heard about Chuck Colson, he part of the infamous Watergate Scandal, aka president Nixon's 'hatchet man.' Colson had been sent to prison after pleading guilty to obstruction of justice. At the time, Gus was serving the fifth year of a five-year sentence which the judge had given him for his attempting to rob a Bridgeport hardware store. Colson's new *Prison Fellowship* ministry was front-page news at the time and every prison population in the country was paying attention.

When Gus told me this story he said that during the night after he'd heard about the Colson ministry he had a dream, a dream like none other he'd ever had. It was as if some kind of angel had come to tell him it was time to give up his life of crime and to follow Colson's lead. The dream was so vivid, so real, that it actually frightened Gus. The next day, while he was having lunch in the prison mess hall, the prison chaplain came by and told everyone there would be a video showing in the mess hall that very evening, a video produced by Colson's team.

I thought it was significant that Gus—who had never before even thought about talking to a chaplain—decided to watch that video. And watch it he did, along with another dozen prisoners. Gus said that when the video was over, most of these tough guys had tears in their eyes. The video was mostly about Jesus, what kind of man He was, His public ministry and, of course, all the events leading up to His crucifixion and resurrection. Near the end of the video Colson comes on, knowing that his audience is made up of men who probably have never set foot in a church, and he challenges them: Start reading your bible; if you don't have one, go to the prison library and find one. Talk to your chaplain, that's what he's here for. Get to know Jesus Christ, that's what He wants you to do. Try to be the kind of man He was. Millions of others have done that, you can too. And eventually you'll know and trust Jesus well enough to ask Him to come into your life. Then you can claim Him as your Lord and Savior and that, friend, is your personal, guaranteed passport to Heaven.

Gus was so inspired by that fifty-minute video that the next day he asked to see the chaplain. He'd never before visited the prison chapel but from that day on, he never missed a Sunday service. And when it came time for his release from prison, he took his mustering-out money, rented an apartment within walking distance of the local Lutheran church and began looking for a job.

Despite the fact that he had spent all that time in prison, Gus was not what you would call 'poor.' He certainly knew the value of money and whenever he was able to do so, he made deposits to his savings account. That account was worth about fifty thousand dollars when he was released and with that kind of security to fall back on he took his time looking for work, this time *honest* work. Just before Gus left the prison, the warden gave him a 'letter of recommendation,' a to-whom-it-may-concern state-ment which told the reader that—in the opinion of the prison's staff—Gus was fully rehabilitated and could be trusted.

He wanted to find a job within walking distance of his apartment; no point in looking for a used car, not yet. There were several gas stations that fit that description, a Standard Oil, a Shell and a Texaco. Gus spoke with the managers of each and was given a job at the Standard Oil station. The manager told him he'd be pumping gas and washing windshields for openers and he'd better be nice to his customers. After two weeks on the job, Gus had learned how to operate the shop's hoist and he could change and repair a flat tire in fifteen minutes. The next step up was the oil change, and a complete under-the-hood inspection. So it wasn't long before the manager realized that Gus was very good at what he was doing, good enough, probably, to run the place by himself on Sundays, when his boss expected the fewest customers.

So now what? Worship service or the job? The Lutheran church had an 'early bird' service that began at 0800 and ended by 0915. Gus could rush home, change clothes and make it to the Standard Oil station no later than ten o'clock. After six months of this routine, the local Standard Oil distributor had come to know Gus well enough that he offered him his own station, in another part of the city. This station was bigger, it had a six-man work force and it operated 24/7, every day of the year. Gus took

the job, no questions asked, and he stayed with it for three more years, three years of 'honest work,' for the first time in his life.

§

I believe I've made the point more than once, that my grandfather—despite his many poor choices—was a bright guy and a hard worker. During those three years with Standard Oil, he probably saved the company tens of thousands of dollars, just by doing the little things that can make any business more efficient. And the company's upper echelon noticed this and decided to ask him to join their headquarters staff in New York City.

The move to the Big Apple was barely a stone's throw from Bridgeport but the cultural distance was, well, light years. Now that he was an *executive*, Gus had to wear a necktie, a clean shirt (every day) and a three-piece suit. And shined, black shoes. Fortunately, the company gave him a month's salary in advance with which he was able to rent a modest apartment and do the necessary shopping.

Gus soon settled in to what became the most challenging and interesting work he had ever done. He got along well with his co-workers and they with him. He was assigned to the public relations department, probably owing to his years in and out of prison during which he befriended all kinds of people, good and bad. It was a good job but Gus began to think about his having to live alone. Most of his co-workers were married, had children, even grandchildren. Sometimes, Gus had to admit to himself that his experience with 'Hilda' was still the real hang-up in his life, even though it had been many years since she disappeared with all that money.

His Christian life was complicated by the fact that there were no Lutheran churches on Manhattan Island. But he was able to drive to Bridgeport, at least once each month, and worship at its Lutheran church.

He made it a point to try to be there on the first Sunday, knowing that he could receive Holy Communion at that time. The bread and the wine meant a lot to Gus, those sacred elements had become an important part of his life.

Gus stayed on with Standard Oil until his retirement, at age sixty-five. That event was reported in *The Wall Street Journal*, Section C, page 4, a small, routine announcement that may have been the final turning point in the life of Gustav Bjorsi.

As Gus related this part of his story, he used the word *serendipity*, but we quickly agreed it was more likely his guardian angel at work. As it happened, there was a man living in Bridgeport who had been—many years earlier—incarcerated in the state prison at the same time Gus was there; and they had become good friends. After his release, Jimmy Blackwell went back to school, earned a degree in accounting and set up shop as a Certified Public Accountant. As a CPA, he became a regular WSJ reader and that was how he learned of his old friend's retirement. Jimmy phoned the Standard Oil headquarters in New York, explained his relationship with Gus and asked if they could give him Gus' phone number.

Well, it was more than 'old home week' when these two men reconnected. Gus told Jimmy he was about to move back to Bridgeport but he hadn't yet decided what part of the city he wanted to live in. Did Jimmy have any ideas about that? Jimmy told him he'd been living in the Bridgeport Covenant Village for the past three years, had long ago become a Christian and he was certain that Gus would absolutely love the place. And, lucky for Gus, there were at least two vacant apartments that he could visit, then decide.

A month later, Gus became a resident of the village and began making new friends. Jimmy quickly became the closest of these and he and Gus spent many hours together, reliving their lives. Jimmy was surprised to learn that Gus had never married but after learning about 'Hilda,' and how that experience had impacted Gus' psyche, he understood. But Jimmy wanted Gus to understand that just about every resident in the village had a story of pain, sorrow, misunderstanding or betrayal. Gus was by no means alone and his feelings of inadequacy were perfectly normal.

Then one evening, in the village dining room, Jimmy invited Helen Blackwell to join him and Gus. Helen had lost her husband some ten years earlier and after moving to the village had become one of the more active residents. She led a weekly bible study, served on the Residents' Council and often participated in Sunday worship services. They joked that Helen was dining with two ex-cons and yet she didn't feel threatened! She was fascinated by Gus' accounts of his experiences—he never mentioned 'Hilda,' of course—and wanted to learn as much as Gus was willing to share.

I'm sure Jimmy Blackwell never thought of himself as a match-maker but, truth be told, Gus and Helen fell in love and began talking about marriage. Gus still had those bad feelings and he wasn't convinced that marrying Helen would be the right thing to do. He shared his concern with Jimmy who then suggested that Gus see the village chaplain. Over the course of several meetings, Gus told the chaplain most of what I've written but he was really torn about marrying Helen. And this seemed to me to be the ideal situation for the on-campus BeFriender ministry to step in.

The chaplain told Gus about BeFrienders. He said he knew a man who would be more than happy to listen to Gus. And that's all he would do; listen. He would never offer advice but by listening to whatever Gus wanted to talk about, chances were very good that Gus would find within himself the healing he needed.

That's how my grandfather met Bill Barstow, a man about the same age and himself a widower. I never knew exactly how many times Bill and Gus got together but within a few months it became clear that the healing was happening. Gus was regaining his self-image and it showed; his closest friends could see the difference.

§

I was there at the wedding when Grandpa married Helen. That was three years ago and I doubt I've ever seen a happier pair. Both of them told me they loved each other just as much as they loved Jesus and they wanted to share that love with anyone who would listen. And, to be sure, many did listen.

It was just two weeks ago that I received a call from the village chaplain. He knew that I am Grandpa's only next of kin and I should be the first to hear the bad news. My grandfather died in the village health center, after experiencing a massive heart attack. The doctor said went quickly, no pain, and—knowing my grandfather—certainly no regrets.

CHAPTER 6

Cheryl

§

ON THE SECOND DAY OF January, 2014, Linda Mason walked into her small office at *The Christian Evangelist*. It was a Thursday morning, the day after the year-end celebrations, and most of the magazine's small staff were taking a few days off, so the office would be nearly empty. But Linda had a column to write, holidays or no holidays. For the past year she had been doing monthly articles for the magazine's Human Interest pages. She loved her job and if one could believe the Letters to the Editor column, her stories were among the magazine's most-read. She thought her current assignment might become the most interesting and challenging of all, talking to and then writing about a seventy-five-year-old grandmother. Cheryl Jameson's story certainly was unusual. And Linda intended to write it.

§

Thinking back on it, she had to wonder if her guardian angle had arranged the whole thing. Linda lived in San Rafael, north of the Golden Gate Bridge, and there had been a spectacular, four-alarm house fire not two miles from her home. A radio bulletin gave her some of the details and she sensed there might be a story, so she drove to the scene, arriving just as the blaze had been put under control. One of the first responders told her that the only casualty had been a nine-year old pet poodle. The dog was in the temporary care of the home's owner, who got out safely, but the dog was lost. The owner was terribly distraught over the loss of the animal because it wasn't hers; she had been caring for it for a close friend who was away on vacation, that friend being the same Cheryl Jameson. Later, when Linda checked Jameson's name against the magazine's database, she discovered that this was *the* Cheryl Jameson, many years ago one of San Francisco's most well-known personalities.

Next stop: the magazine's library. She found the Marin County telephone directory and there it was, *Jameson, Cheryl, 628 536 4958; 6597 Overview Drive, Apt 5503.*

§

Cheryl didn't answer the call; her voice mail did, saying that she was away for two weeks. 'Pease contact the Covenant Village central switchboard: 628 412 3000.'

'What's that all about,?' Linda wondered. She checked the reverse directory and found that the 3000 number belonged to the San Pablo Covenant Village. That led her to her computer where she Googled the name and *viola!* 'Now we're getting somewhere.'

San Pablo Covenant Village, one of a dozen Covenant Retirement Community facilities, headquartered in Chicago, Ill. San Pablo village, established in 2005 and with a lovely view overlooking San Pablo Bay, includes residential living apartments, assisted living facilities, a health center, a lodge and recreation center that includes dining facilities for up to 400 residents. Not lost on Linda was *sponsorship*, the Evangelical Covenant Church of America. So Cheryl Jameson almost certainly is a Christian and that means her story belongs in *my* magazine—if, a big IF— she's willing to let me publish it.

Linda decided to write Cheryl a brief note, expressing her sympathy for the lost poodle, how she learned of it, and would Cheryl be willing to talk to Linda? There might be a human-interest story for her magazine, whose readership includes most of Central California, especially in churches and other Christian organizations.

Now Linda had two weeks to wait for a response. She used some of that time to learn as much as she could about the subject of her next story. She visited the San Rafael library, displayed her press card to the receptionist and asked if she could have access to archived articles, mostly likely on microfiche film, covering the post-World War II period, 1946 onward. Newspaper society pages would be of most interest, judging by what Linda had learned from office colleagues who thought they remembered the name, Cheryl Jameson.

§

Fortunately, the librarian was able to find a working microfiche reader, after explaining to Linda that the library had very few requests for this kind of research. But, as old as the system was, it worked well enough for Linda to find what she was looking for. It was an article on the society page of the *San Francisco Sentinel*, published on June 12, 1958.

Beautiful Debs
by Loraine Dickerson

The Presidio, June 12

If you were fortunate enough to receive an invitation to the Presidio's June 11 debutante cotillion—they invite me only because I write nice things about them—you would have been impressed. Three beautiful eighteen year olds, each of them with more talent than seems fair. No one voted, but I'd give my nod to Cheryl Jameson, a stunning blonde whose piano plays just about everything Beethoven ever wrote. Her proud parents were there, of course, as were the parents of Cheryl's escort, Jim Olson. Jim is a handsome, young ROTC officer presently attending Stanford University. It was said that the two plan to marry but not until he receives his commission and a permanent assignment.

Cheryl has now finished her last semester at the Saint Jude Academy, one of San Francisco's most prestigious girls' schools. Apparently most of the guests at the event—held in the officers' club—are abstemious souls because the bar served only soft drinks. And with the academy's senior lector—Fr Michael Flannigan—in attendance, one would suppose most are Christians.

The Jameson family prefers to keep a low profile but it's no secret that they continue to control seventy percent ownership of California's largest and most lucrative hardware chain, Jamesons, Inc. Interestingly, it was—ages ago—'gold money' that got them started. One of the very early Jamesons made a small fortune in the 1850s gold rush, then decided the hardware business was here to stay.

I was able to speak with Cheryl, briefly, and she told me that she has been accepted at Stanford and will begin her studies there in September. She impressed me as a young woman who is far beyond her years: easy to talk to, beautiful, calm, smart and supremely self-confident. She'll be more than welcome on that Stanford campus!

That was more than Linda had expected and much more than enough to prepare for her first visit—assuming, of course—that Cheryl Jameson responded to her note.

Two weeks later she did respond. In her note, Linda had included her office phone number but wasn't at her desk when the call came in. Her voice mail revealed a reluctant but curious senior citizen: *Ms. Mason. You should understand that nowadays I'm a very private person and I don't know about talking to a reporter. But call me when you can and we'll see if we can work something out. 628 536 4958.*

An hour later, the two women did connect. Cheryl agreed that Linda could come to her apartment the next day, at ten in the morning. Then, if they wished, they could have lunch together in the community dining room. And although Linda thought of herself as an experienced and competent reporter, she was about to be challenged as never before: learning and writing about the life of woman who at one time had everything she could wish for, absent the happiness that had eluded her for ten, painful years.

§

It's my granddaughter. She's pregnant. The man refuses to have anything to do with her. He says she's just like any other prostitute; she deserves it.

Linda had taken two smart phones with her to the interview and asked Cheryl if it would be okay to record their conversations. She promised not to publish anything in the magazine before giving Cheryl opportunity to go over the manuscript. But these words about her granddaughter seemed to sum up the ongoing tragedy that had been nagging her for a very long time.

When she arrived at Cheryl's fifth floor apartment, Linda introduced herself, showed Cheryl her press card and *Christian Evangelist* ID photo. She had thought to bring a copy of the *San Francisco Sentinel*'s 1958 article describing Cheryl's debut at the Presidio's officers' club. It was the perfect ice-breaker, reminding Cheryl that Linda had done her homework and could be thought of as a sympathetic, Christian friend.

As she listened to more of the recordings, Linda realized the interview had been an emotional strain for both of them, each coming to tears more than once. After listening to Cheryl's story, they agreed to ease up and have lunch together in the village dining room, Linda using the opportunity for follow-up questions, to be sure she had everything exactly right. Back in her office, she decided to write the story in four parts, one part each month. Part One looked like this.

GOD'S GRACE WORKING

PART ONE
by Linda Mason

This is the story of a seventy-five year old grandmother, a woman whose name at one time was well known to many Bay Area residents. She has consented to the publication of her story, believing that other Christians might be encouraged by learning about her life experiences.

It was in June 1958 that Cheryl Jameson first appeared on the society pages of San Francisco's newspapers. As she cheerfully acknowledges, she was born 'with a silver spoon in my mouth,' as that expression was used in those days. Debutante cotillions were standard fare at the time and the U.S. Army's Presidio hosted its share of them. Cheryl, by nature a rather shy young woman, reluctantly participated in this cotillion for two reasons. One, because her parents expected it of her and, two, she was escorted to the event by Jim Olson, the man she eventually married, an ROTC officer who was enrolled at Stanford University.

The following September, Cheryl joined her intended by enrolling in Stanford University's School of Music. She already was an accomplished pianist but she aspired to better things—perhaps, some day, a position with the San Francisco symphony orchestra.

The day following the Japanese attack on Pearl Harbor in December, 1941, Cheryl's father, William Jameson III, volunteered for service in the U.S. Army. By war's end he was in command of the army's Logistics Operations Center at Fort Lewis in Washington state. Mustered out in October 1945, he returned to San Francisco as a reserve colonel, rejoined his wife and daughter and moved his family into the Presidio's officers' quarters.

Cheryl was only five years old at the time and had just been enrolled in the kindergarten component of San Francisco's all-girls Saint Jude Academy. Her parents had insisted on a Catholic school environment and Saint Jude proved to be a perfect venue for Cheryl's schooling.

By the time Cheryl was in high school, her teachers had recognized her natural aptitudes and they urged her to study at least one foreign language. When she left Saint Jude she was nearly fluent in French.

As Cheryl described her growing-up years, she spoke of herself as 'the typical army brat,' and she thought it not unusual that she would marry another army brat, Jim Olson, himself the son of a U.S. Army brigadier general.

Cheryl's marriage to Jim was one of the city's social highlights. She had decided to speed up her course work at Stanford so that she could graduate with Jim, in June 1961. She had always dreamed of being a 'June bride,' and she wasn't disappointed. It was a given that she and Jim would be married at the Presidio's officers' club but when Cheryl's parents arranged for the Archbishop of San Francisco, Fr. Damon Blackwell, to preside over the ceremony, the story appeared in every newspaper in California.

For their honeymoon, the newlyweds chose the island of Maui. Preparing for the wedding, recording the many gifts, writing thank-you notes, all of this had taken its toll and Cheryl and Jim wanted to get away and relax. They booked a five-star hotel in Kaanapali, played eighteen holes of golf each day, enjoyed the hotel's swimming pool and restaurants and—their pre-planned highlight—drove a rented Jeep around the island to visit Charles Lindberg's burial site on the grounds of the Palapala Ho'omau Church in the village of Kipahulu. It was an emotional and memorable experience for these Christian newlyweds as they read the famous aviator's epitaph etched into a simple gravestone, a quotation from Psalm 139:9-10 *If I take the wings of the dawn, and dwell in the uttermost parts of the sea, even there Your hand will lead me ... C.A.L.*

Not long after they returned to San Francisco, Cheryl realized that she was pregnant, not an unexpected discovery. She and Jim had talked about a family and, at least 'for openers'—as she put it—they would be happy to have just one child, especially a girl. And so it was. Nine months later, Cheryl gave birth to their first child and named her Cheryl Marie. In her later years, Cheryl Marie was to become the first of many tragedies in the life of Cheryl Jameson.

More next month.

§

God's Grace Working

PART TWO
by Linda Mason

She was now Cheryl Jameson Olson, or 'Mrs. James Olson' as some of her correspondents addressed her, and Cheryl, Jim and their infant daughter found themselves at Jim's first posting abroad, at the U.S. consulate general in Quebec City. Although not as proficient in French as Cheryl, Jim Olson had studied the language in high school and as the consulate's junior military attaché he wouldn't be expected to use French very often. Nor did he have the representational responsibilities that were expected of the consulate's senior officers.

Owing to his junior rank, Jim and Cheryl were on a limited U.S. military budget and were unable to ship to Quebec City all of their household furnishings. Cheryl insisted that her baby grand piano should be part of their family and so she paid for the shipment herself. When word of this got around the consulate, those who didn't already know, now were aware that this young woman was not only talented but determined. Cheryl also took it upon herself to upgrade their housing allowance, moving the family into a three bedroom home located within walking distance of the consulate.

Not long after they were settled in their new home, Jim and Cheryl had their first argument, a 'mini-quarrel' as she described it. At issue was whether Cheryl should be a stay-at-home mom or be able to move about the city on her own, whenever she wished. They decided to hire an English-speaking French Canadian au pair, a bi-lingual woman who could be at home with infant Cheryl Marie three days a week. That would expose the child to two languages in the same household and if Jim's assignment ran for the expected three years, their daughter—at the tender age of three—might well be proficient in both French and English.

Jim's boss, Consul-General Peter Crockett, was a thirty year State Department veteran, fluent in French and German, and a no-nonsense supervisor who expected his staff to do everything by the book and on time. As the senior American diplomat in Quebec Province he had a demanding appointments schedule and even heavier representational responsibilities. And he was a widower, having lost his wife five years earlier. He soon learned about this beautiful, talented newbie, Cheryl Olson, and after inviting her to lunch one afternoon Cheryl found herself in the enviable position of being the Consul-General's hostess for the indefinite future. When Jim first heard of it he was skeptical, but then Cheryl reminded him that than man was old enough to be her father, so not to worry. Still, the responsibility was an important one and Cheryl found herself at the center of the consulate's social events program, planning and hosting luncheons and other events nearly every weekend.

As Cheryl related these events she told me that for the first time in her life she had become aware that her talent, good looks, financial security and social graces carried an unexpected—to her—level of responsibility. As the wife of a United States official, and after thee years as the consulate's unofficial hostess, she had become one of the more visible American personalities in all of Canada. As such, she felt both proud and somewhat intimidated. Her principal concern was that this new lifestyle might detract from what was most important—raising her daughter to the same standards to which she was accustomed.

In hindsight, she told me, those three years passed by all too quickly. They were happy times, as both she and husband Jim made many friends, not only in Quebec's diplomatic community, but throughout the city. And, as important, they were able to watch their daughter grow from toddler to a precocious three-year old child who spoke better French than either of her parents.

Before leaving Quebec, now-lieutenant James Olson received his orders to his new assignment: The Pentagon, as senior aide to Lt. General Timothy Barcroft, in charge of army logistics support for the European Theater.

This time the army paid for all of the move, including Cheryl's baby grand piano. They chose to live in Alexandria, Virginia, no more than a twenty minute commute to Jim's new office and they decided they could afford *two* automobiles. Cheryl chose an off-white Mercedes convertible and the more practical Jim settled for a new Ford Explorer.

But, most important of all: Not far from their new home in Alexandria, they found a preschool run by three Catholic nuns who were more than willing to accept three-going-on-four Cheryl Marie.

Jim's Pentagon tour passed as quickly as had the one in Quebec, but it was different. General Barcroft visited the several European capitals twice each year. He was a hands-on general and insisted on face-to-face meetings with his subordinates. And as the general's senior aide, Jim Olson went with him, 'carrying his briefcase,' as he called it. If the Pentagon tour did anything for Jim's career, it exposed him to the real world of United States diplomacy: maintaining—and, where possible, improving—cordial relations with America's NATO allies and in the process assuring that the Soviet Union behaved itself.

General Barcroft liked Jim and said so, officially, in his written PE's, or Performance Evaluations. And at the end of the three years it was, as Jim had wished, back to San Francisco, this time as a newly-minted Lt. Colonel who would be second-in-command of the entire Presidio complex.

And what a thrill for Cheryl. The Presidio assignment meant that six-year-old Cheryl Marie could go to the same girls' school that Mom had attended, Saint Jude. And so it was.

§

In my conversations with Cheryl, she tended to 'fast-forward' over the next fifteen years, mentioning just two assignments that she and her husband thought were significant. Husband Jim, by now an Army colonel, saw that his reputation had made its way back to the U.S. State Department and they sent word to the Pentagon, suggesting that Jim be assigned to either London or Paris, as one of the embassy's senior military attachés. The London stint was wonderful, working in an English-speaking environment and within a month or so of their arrival, the embassy's cultural attaché realized that Cheryl and Jim could make wonderful entertainment, Cheryl at the piano and Jim with his better-than-good baritone voice. By the time their tour was over, Cheryl had lost count of how many times they had performed at the embassy's many weekend soirees.

Near the close of their London tour, they received orders for a direct transfer to Paris, the personnel office in Washington knowing that Cheryl's French was nearly perfect and Jim's good enough. Virtually the same pattern was repeated there, with Jim and Cheryl doing a good bit of entertaining, until the last month of their tour: Something happened that would change Cheryl's life forever.

♩

At the time, Cheryl Marie was married to Kelly Adams, or 'Mr. Wonderful,' as she described him in her many letters to her parents. And they had a five-year old daughter, Cheryl Anne. The Kellys were determined to fly to Paris and re-introduce Cheryl Anne to her grandparents.

It was joyful reunion at Orly international airport. Jim and Cheryl, because of their travels, had seen their granddaughter only once before, when she was barely two. Now, at five, they could see that she would one day become a beautiful woman, just like her mother.

Jim had been able to get two tickets to the Moulin Rouge cabaret, assuming his daughter would want to share the city's most popular night club with her husband. After overnighting with Jim and Cheryl, Kelly arranged for a cab to take them to the event the following afternoon. While they were away, Cheryl Anne could get to know her grandparents; it would be a good time for bonding.

Cheryl was sobbing as she told me this part of her story. That taxi cab never arrived at the Moulin Rouge. It was broadsided by a fully-loaded, out-of-control eighteen wheeler and the driver, Kelly and Cheryl Marie died instantly.

More next month.

God's Grace Working

Part Three
by Linda Mason

How do you explain to a five-year-old that her parents aren't coming home—ever?

The moment the word of this heart-breaking tragedy spread throughout the building, there was an outpouring of emotional support, especially from the embassy wives. Some of them had been through similar trials, were good friends of Jim's and Cheryl's, and offered them as much moral support as they could have hoped for.

Another huge help: The American embassy in Paris employed a large staff, including—in its cultural affairs division—Dr. Ramsey Donovan, an experienced psychologist/therapist who happened also to be a Christian. Jim and Cheryl had known Dr. Donovan for some time, they attended the same church and were good friends. Within thirty minutes of hearing the news, he telephoned Cheryl and offered to do what he could with/for Cheryl Anne.

Cheryl knew from a number of letters that her daughter had never written a will, she of that 'invincible youth' notion, nor had her husband. In a way that made the chore easier. She and Jim decided to have the remains cremated in Paris. The urns could go back to the states with Cheryl and Jim, who already had decided to cut their tour short and get back to San Francisco and the Presidio just as soon as they could arrange it.

'It's a good example of how God works in mysterious ways,' she told me. "Without Dr. Donovan's help, I don't know what we would have done.' Jim and Cheryl were able to have Donovan present when they broke the news to their granddaughter. 'It was the most difficult thing I've ever done. Both of us were hurting. She had just lost her mother and I had just lost my daughter.'

The hugging and weeping continued far into the evening when, finally, little Cheryl Anne, emotionally exhausted, fell asleep. After carrying Cheryl Anne into their guest bedroom and tucking her in, Cheryl, Jim and the doctor returned to the living room, sat down and began discussing next steps. The doctor assured them they could leave Paris at any time; he would endorse travel orders that would specify 'family emergency' with the stipulation that the two would not be returning to Paris.

Jim, for his part, had already decided to send a message to the Presidio, explaining what had happened and alerting the base commanding officer that he likely would arrive within the next three weeks. Then he placed a phone call to the base personnel officer, a man he had known for years, to learn if there were any openings that Jim might fill. He had already served thirty years and could retire any time he wished, but it would be most satisfying to do one more tour at his favorite post.

Jim's call to the personnel officer paid off. The Presidio's on-base housing had one open unit, a three bedroom rambler, and Jim's rank would give him priority. The family could move in as soon as they arrived. The third bedroom would be for Cheryl Anne—but not for long. Her grandmother already had decided that she and Jim were too old to be raising a five-year-old, precocious and rambunctious little girl. Cheryl had gone on line and found an orphanage, *Jesus' Little Children*, operated by three Catholic nuns and located on Fulton Street, just north of Golden Gate Park. That put it within a ten minutes' drive of the Presidio. It was an expensive facility, to be sure, but money was not the issue. It was her granddaughter's welfare that concerned her. She sent an email to the nuns, telling them as much of the story as she thought necessary, and asked to be placed on their waiting list.

The threesome arrived at San Francisco's international airport three weeks after the Paris tragedy and taxied directly to the Presidio. The rambler had been refurbished and its kitchen stocked with enough food for a few days. And there was a note for Jim, taped to the fridge door, from his friend, the base personnel officer: 'When convenient, please come to my office. I have good news.'

As Cheryl recounted this story, she told me this 'good news' was the last good news to reach her family for a very long time. Jim leaned that the Presidio's commanding officer was about to retire and that he, Jim, could have the job if he wanted it. Well, of course he wanted it. It meant a slight increase in pay and, best of all, the base commander's quarters: a beautiful home sited on a hill overlooking the Pacific Ocean.

§

Placing Cheryl Anne in that orphanage was one of the most difficult things Cheryl had even done. Both she and Jim had tried to reason with the child, offering her all the reasons for their having to do it. Finally, one of the nuns, Sister Margaret Cavanaugh, offered a solution. She could arrange to have Cheryl Anne share a room with a girl her age, they could share their meals together and, best of all, her grandmother would come to visit at least three times a week. And, they would go to mass together each Sunday.

The sister's 'formula' worked well enough for the first two years, but then an eight-year-old boy took a liking to Cheryl Anne, and she to him. The nuns thought nothing of it at the time; they'd seen more than one example of puppy love among their wards. Cheryl, after meeting the lad, decided it was time that her granddaughter had a playmate of the opposite sex. Little did she know, then, that this 'playmate' would soon become a major disruption in the activities of the orphanage and the life of Cheryl Anne.

Actually, he lied about his age, or his estranged uncle did when he dropped him off at the orphanage. His name was Billy Goodwin and he was ten, not eight. And he had friends 'on the outside,' as he later bragged to Cheryl Anne. Friends who had other friends who knew some of the pushers in the Bay Area. At first it was just a drag or two on a marijuana joint, enough to get Cheryl Anne to 'feel real good.' But it wasn't long before she was hooked. And Billy knew that her grandmother had tons of money. Not only did Billy have the right connections but he was clever, too. He made certain that when Cheryl Anne's grandmother came to visit, Cheryl Anne was sober, or nearly so, so that Grandma wouldn't notice.

Little Cheryl Anne wasn't the only child in that orphanage to fall victim to Billy's charms. Even some of the older children became interested in his fast-talking spiel. At night, when everyone should have been sleeping, they would gather in Billy's room and listen to him prattle on about the joys of marijuana.

When Cheryl told me this part of her story, she admitted to feeling the fool when she finally realized what was going on, right under her nose.

By now, Cheryl Anne was nearly twelve, beginning to show the early signs of womanhood. But she was still hooked on drugs, experimenting with some of the more dangerous ones. And the nuns noticed, too, and it wasn't long before Billy was asked to leave the orphanage, sent back to his reluctant uncle and never heard from again. But the damage had been done; Cheryl Anne would never be the same.

§

Meanwhile, Cheryl's life at home took a wrong turn. Jim, now the Presidio's commanding officer, had decided to retire after one more year. He enjoyed his job but the strain of responsibility was taking its toll. And he wasn't feeling well, complaining to Cheryl of a 'funny feeling' in his abdominal area. After the examination, the Presidio's senior medical officer suspected it was cancer but rather than sharing his opinion with Jim, he ordered tests to be conducted at San Francisco's Saint Francis Memorial Hospital. And it *was* cancer, one of the most virulent and fast-moving kinds. Within a month, Brigadier General James Olson was gone.

Cheryl was now a widow whose remaining years would be devoted to her granddaughter's uncertain future.

More next month.

GOD'S GRACE WORKING

PART FOUR
by Linda Mason

Jim Olson was laid to rest in the Presidio's cemetery, with full military honors. Cheryl Anne, now fifteen, was standing beside her grandmother when the honor guard presented Cheryl the folded American flag.

Somewhere in the distance a bugler played Taps. When the service was over, the two returned to Cheryl's home, there to talk about what was likely to happen next.

Cheryl Anne had nearly outgrown the orphanage; she could move out at any time, but what then? Their first decision: She would stay on for one more year, continue her schooling at St. Jude's Academy but she would move in to the academy's dormitory. Cheryl, for her part, already had decided she needed to move on. Staying at the Presidio, with all its attendant memories, would be too much. She and Jim already had talked about this and after hearing about the Covenant Retirement Communities' San Pablo Covenant Village, they visited the campus, did a tour with its marketing director, and put down a deposit. Now, all she needed to do was to check her place on the waiting list.

She assured her granddaughter that even though it would be a longer drive, she would visit her at least three times a week. And, with a two-bedroom apartment at the village, Cheryl Anne could stay with her grandmother over weekends.

Having just attended her husband's graveside service, Cheryl thought it the wrong time to ask Cheryl Anne about her drug dependency. Each of them was suffering, quietly and in her own way; not a good time to talk about a difficult subject. But it was something that had to be addressed. She knew there was a chaplain serving at San Pablo Covenant. Perhaps, in good time, she could help.

§

The best part of her move from the Presidio to San Pablo Covenant Village: Cheryl found enough room in her apartment for her baby grand piano. It was a squeeze, to be sure, but rather than be the 'lonely widow,' she was determined to make the place as much like home as possible.

No surprise, her reputation had preceded her and at her first Residents' Council meeting she was welcomed with warm applause. At that same meeting the RC president asked her if she would like to play those piano parts that would be needed at each Sunday service. Of course she agreed and learned that her first rehearsal would be the following Thursday. Then, the following Sunday, the campus congregation gathered in its Fellowship Hall and Cheryl found herself at the keyboard; but not *any* keyboard. This was a Steinway concert grand piano, the world's best. She had never played one but after the rehearsal she handled it like the artist she was.

Following the service, Cheryl was introduced to the campus chaplain, a woman in her late fifties who had served in Covenant churches throughout California, Arizona and Oregon. Mary Magruder was in her fifth year of service at San Pablo and she asked Cheryl, as she was leaving the service, if they could meet in her office the next day.

At nine in the morning, Cheryl walked into Mary Magruder's office. Magruder told her she was aware of Cheryl's problems with her granddaughter; apparently that kind of information reaches a chaplain's ears rather quickly. After that bridge was crossed, Cheryl told her the whole story: Drugs, promiscuity, boyfriends who had been dishonest and misleading, her ongoing and never-successful search for someone who could really love her, and now this.

'I just learned that she's pregnant. The man refuses to have anything to do with her. He says she's just like any other prostitute; she deserves it. Can you imagine that? Calling my granddaughter a *prostitute?*'

Magruder reminded Cheryl that there was a least one positive in this picture: Her granddaughter was willing to share some very unpleasant truths. How can we build on that?

The two women talked for another ten minutes and then Magruder told Cheryl about the BeFriender ministry, its on-campus history, its principles and practices and—in her opinion—how it might offer Cheryl a workable solution. There was a woman living in the same building as Cheryl; a woman who had been in the BeFriender program since its inception. Her name is Martha McGovern and, like Cheryl, she's a widow. Would Cheryl agree to meet with her?

§

Agree she did and Cheryl met with her BeFriender for the next two months, usually once a week in Cheryl's apartment. McGovern mostly listened to Cheryl's story, occasionally asking a few questions. Then she suggested something she'd never done before, and she would want to talk to the chaplain first, to see if she agreed: Did Cheryl think her granddaughter would be willing to talk to McGovern? If she agreed, then McGovern could hear both sides of the story. Cheryl thought it was a wonderful idea; it might bring about an otherwise unreachable reconciliation.

§

After listening to her grandmother's suggestion, Cheryl Anne reluctantly agreed, promising to 'give it a try,' but no more than that. She had been spending weekends with her grandmother, using the apartment's second bedroom as her home away from home. These weekends were important to both women, giving each of them time to talk, sometimes to weep, but always reminding them how much the loved and needed each other. Still, it was impossible to avoid the subject, Cheryl Anne's pregnancy. She was still in her first month and thought she should have an abortion; that was one of the few things they could *not* agree on, something that Cheryl hoped would come up when her granddaughter began her conversations with Martha McGovern.

Cheryl was aware of the confidentiality code that is so important to the BeFriender ministry. So no matter how curious she might have been about her granddaughter's chats with Martha McGovern, she could only guess. But after a few weeks, she began to sense that Cheryl Anne was changing. She seemed to be more relaxed, the signs of stress gradually disappearing. She couldn't prove it but she was quite certain that Cheryl Anne and Martha were talking about *faith*. Both of them knew that for generations the Jameson family had been committed Christians; why should Cheryl Anne be different?

§

Toward the end of my interview with Cheryl, she told me that Cheryl Anne continued her visits with Martha McGovern for another six months. She decided to keep the baby, a choice made easier by her new relationship with a young man who is the grandson of a San Pablo resident. They had met in the village dining room, and if it wasn't love at first sight it was something pretty close to it. Best of all, for Cheryl, the young man is a Christian and he and Cheryl Anne will be married in the local Covenant Church, just before the baby is due. She understands that the baby and her mother probably will be baptized at the same time.

One more thing before I close this story. Cheryl told me that throughout her adult life she knew she was financially secure, she didn't have to work if she didn't want to, she could buy virtually anything that pleased her. Yet, in her twilight years, she realizes that money can never buy happiness, that it is family and friends who matter most. She knew that, of course, but it was the San Pablo BeFriender ministry that made the difference.

CHAPTER 7
David

§

THEY WERE SITTING AROUND A small campfire, not far from the river's edge. It was too dark to be fishing and someone had already brought out a six pack of cold Heinekens. One of the women provided the skewers, another the Frankfurters, a large can of Bush Beans and a huge bag of potato chips; for dessert, they had marshmallows and graham crackers and could make S'mores. If the fishing wasn't what they'd hoped for, at least they could eat well and then look forward to tomorrow.

It had been a tough day and their stories were few. Cathy, his wife, said she hooked, and lost, a twelve-pound buck steelhead; took out most of her backing and nearly spooled her. She'd been fishing the Bridge pool, one of her favorites. David, her lawyer-husband, usually a better fisherman than the others, didn't say much. He'd been using his new eleven-foot all-graphite spey rod and hadn't yet mastered the technique. He was in the Graveyard pool, a short distance downstream of Spences Bridge and like the rest of the Thompson, the wading was treacherous, the bottom covered with super-slick boulders the size of basketballs. Any kind of misstep and you were very, very wet, even if you were wearing chest-high waders. One fish had nearly taken his foam skater but he missed it, probably a fifteen pounder, judging by what he could see of its dorsal fin.

There were six of them, close Christian friends, two in each motor home. This was dry camping, across the river from the village but still in view of BC's Highway One, the main highway all the way north to the Yukon. You brought everything with you: at least thirty gallons of fresh water, a fully-stocked fridge, even extra toilet paper. The British Columbia wildlife wardens—who monitored the improvised campground—weren't much on fancy stuff; there wasn't even an outhouse. But they didn't care because they knew that even without the usual amenities, the Thompson River attracted more stateside fly fisherman than any other river in the province. You could drive to Spences Bridge from Seattle in no more than six or seven hours. Most folks stayed in the campground maybe two, three days, then headed out for more supplies. Or, if the fishing wasn't to their liking, they might go north, all the way to Smithers. From there, they could fish the Kispiox, the Morice, the Sustut, even the much larger Skeena, if they wanted to drive that far.

David volunteered to make the S'mores and while he did that he spun a yarn they'd heard before; but good enough to repeat. Two years earlier he and Cathy had parked alongside the Kispiox. They had their small Subaru station wagon in tow behind the motor home. Cathy knew the terrain as well as anyone and it was a routine they'd been through many times. David inflated his nine-foot, one-man Achilles raft, hopped in and soon was out of sight. Cathy would meet him in the Subaru at the take-out, about five miles downstream.

Anyone who fished these waters knew that the Kispiox held some of the largest steelhead to be found in British Columbia. Twenty pounds was not uncommon and it had been David's dream to catch and release not one, but *two* of these monster rainbows, if not in one day, then certainly in two. Well, believe it or not—and David tried to convince everyone that this was *not* another 'fish story'—he did just that: a twenty-pound buck the first day and a slightly larger hen the next. David knew he'd get some ribbing when he told this story because there were no witnesses and with a fish that big thrashing around out there and only a nine-weight fly rod for control, taking pictures was impossible.

The campfire eventually flickered out and after praying for a better tomorrow, everyone headed for bed.

§

His name was David McPherson and of course his friends called him Dave. A native Oregonian, David was born in Portland in 1930. A month after his birth his parents had him baptized in the Willamette Valley Covenant Church. The Great Depression hadn't yet reached the West Coast but it soon would, about the time David was entering kindergarten. His parents both taught in Portland's public school District 255. His father taught geometry, algebra, the calculus and physics and his mother worked with the girls, teaching home economics: sewing, cooking, house keeping and home health care. In those days teachers weren't paid very much and in his later years David recalled his father going to the local pawn shop, hocking his gold-plated pocket watch, and from there walking to the grocery store.

David was a big kid, and by the time he was ready to enter high school he had grown to nearly six feet, he weighed about 175 and the high school football coach thought he should join the team. Which he did. In his senior year his Jefferson High School Panthers placed second in the state finals, held in Portland's Multnomah County stadium. David played both offense and defense and as the team's go-to wide receiver he set Oregon state records for total yards and receptions for touchdowns.

About half-way through his senior year, David was trying to decide 'what next?' His father reminded him that as between becoming a lawyer and a doctor, remember this: Many people can go through life without ever having to see a lawyer; not so with doctors. 'But it's your choice.'

Well, for one thing, David didn't think he had the patience to grind through a six-year medical school program. And he thought that, as a lawyer, he'd likely be dealing with more interesting people: people in trouble, people threatened by government bureaucrats, maybe even people accused of crimes who would need a good defense attorney.

Next decision: Where to study for his law degree? As it happened, one of his Panthers teammates hailed from Longview, just across the Columbia River in Washington state. And his sister was going to school at the University of Washington, in Seattle. She had sent her brother pictures of the U-Dub campus: Frosh Pond, the chimes and the observatory on 45th Avenue, Husky Stadium, Hec Edmunson Pavilion on Montlake Boulevard.

For David, Seattle seemed like the 'big city,' at least compared to Portland. He made a few inquiries, talked to his high school principal and decided to head north. His father lent him enough money to pay the school's entry fee, and a little more for the books he would need as a freshman pre-law student. When he arrived on campus, in late September 1947, he went directly to the office of the registrar, signed for the classes he wanted, plunked down the first quarter's tuition and then looked for a place to live.

Fraternities were out, at least for now. Too expensive and David thought it best to avoid the 'I'm-better-than-you' tag that might go with living on Greek Row.

§

It wasn't a 'six-year-grind,' only five, but David received his law degree in June 1952. He ranked third in a Law School class of thirty five and his professors had already identified a Seattle law firm that would take him on as an intern. There was a 'problem,' however. The Korean war was raging at the time, something every male student was much aware of. In his sophomore year, David had decided to apply for a Navy ROTC billet.

That arrangement would help pay his college expenses and in exchange he would be obligated to serve as a reserve naval officer for three years.

His first year with the law firm Duncan, Winfield, James and Tolliver was, as he later called it, 'a very steep learning curve.' The firm gave him more than he could handle, mostly testing him to see how badly he wanted to become a *real* lawyer. The firm's senior partner, Harvey Duncan, was one of the best trial lawyers in Washington State and most of his cases were heard in the King County Superior Court house, on Third Avenue in downtown Seattle. Duncan made certain that David had a seat in the gallery so he could learn by watching and listening.

As he later described it, David thought it was God's hand at work, a 'brotherly bonding' like nothing else: Harvey Duncan's son, Josh, was about David's age and he was clerking for a lawyer in another law firm. The two of them had lunch together and David learned, for the first time, about fly fishing. Josh Duncan had been fly fishing Washington's coastal rivers since he was fifteen years old, nearly every one of them, all the way from the Hoko River in the northwestern tip of the state down to the Naselle, only a few miles north of the mouth of the Columbia.

Well, you can imagine what these two new friends did the following weekend. They went fishing, together. Josh had a back-up pair of boot-foot waders, two spare fly rods, one reel with enough line to give David some experience at casting a fly line, and a pocket book full of flies, mostly steelhead patterns: Green Butt Skunk, General Practitioner, Skykomish Sunrise, Doc Spratley, and two Muddler Minnows.

It was late August and Josh decided they should drive up Highway Two to the village of Skykomish, on the South Fork of the Skykomish River. Even if they never touched a fish the trip would be worth it; some of the most spectacular mountain scenery in the western United States. Josh had fished this river—always in late summer—many times and knew all the back roads and tracks over which they could walk to the river's edge.

David's early attempts at fly casting were about what any rookie would expect but he caught on quickly, his earlier athleticism a big plus. Before the day was over he was putting the fly out there at least thirty feet, sometimes farther than that, with a back cast in a tight, smooth loop. Josh hooked one bright steelhead, the fish ran off about thirty yards of line before he broke water and in one spectacular jump, threw the hook and was on his way back to the ocean.

Well, the obvious thing to say is that David was 'hooked,' and he certainly was. And it wasn't lost on him that Josh's father was David's boss. Would he look kindly on his new intern's fascination with fly fishing? Only time would tell.

§

After his first year with the firm, David's status was upgraded from intern to junior associate. He had to get some business cards printed with his name and firm's logo and he was now making enough money to move into his own apartment, on Queen Anne Hill, a short bus ride to the firm's offices. Although his parents didn't like it, he decided he would make Seattle his home. He had purchased a very used Chevy pick up truck and he could drive to Portland in three hours, go to church with his parents and get back to Seattle in time for work Monday morning.

One of his reasons for staying in Seattle? He had already joined the Washington Fly Fishing Club, the WFFC as it was known, the oldest fly fishing club west of the Mississippi River. This was to be something new. Most WFFC members fished lakes and small streams for rainbow trout. And they held at least one outing every summer, the most popular being at Lake Chopaka, high in the mountains of Okanagan County and a fly-fishing-only piece of water. For this kind of fishing David needed some new 'stuff,' mainly a float tube, with waders and flippers. And as one *sits* in a float tube, he had to learn to cast from a sitting position. He made his first trip to Chopaka with his friend, Josh, and while there he met a young woman, herself a pretty decent fly fisher. And, wouldn't you know? She was single—and *very* pretty.

Her name was Cathy Williams and she worked in Seattle for a start-up advertizing firm. She had finished her studies at Seattle Pacific University, with a degree in counseling. She said she was a committed Christian who loved the out of doors and she was thinking about trying to organize a fly fishing club for *women*, something that, at that time, had never been done, anywhere. Cathy, David and Josh dined in the back of David's pickup: beer, pretzels, a large can of Pinto beans, and a stick of salami. Before returning to her lady friends and their four-person tent, she told the two that she was living in an apartment at the foot of Queen Anne Hill. On weekends—when she wasn't fishing—she liked to visit the kids who were going to nearby St. Anne's, a private Christian school for girls up to age twelve.

During the long drive back to Seattle, Josh could sense that David had taken a real liking to Cathy and that, very likely, he would be seeing more of her. That might even interfere with his weekend fishing trips; better still, the two could go fishing together!

Fast forward now to October 1955. The not-to-be-denied David McPherson and Catherine Marie Williams are married by the senior chaplain at Seattle Pacific University. The invited guests included many of the WFFC members and about fifteen of Cathy's fly fishing girl friends. The newlyweds' honeymoon destination: The Riverside Inn in Winthrop, Washington, with the Methow River just down the road. It is steelhead season on the Methow, one of the most picturesque rivers in the state, whose fish have journeyed more than five hundred miles from the Pacific Ocean. It will be catch-and-release, each of the two carrying a camera to record the other's success.

And there were many pictures. Between the two of them, they landed, photographed and released ten steelhead, each one a wild fish weighing eight pounds or more. After each day on the river they returned to the hotel's nearly-empty dining room, finding most of the village asleep. But not these two. The menu was always the same: A Columbia Valley merlot, T-bone steaks medium-rare, sautéed fresh veggies, and chocolate muse for dessert. Then to bed, to dream about each other and tomorrow.

§

After a year of watching his boss at work in the court room, David thought he was ready. He had yet to try a case but he had learned the names and faces of many of Seattle's best lawyers. One Monday morning he found a note on his desk, informing him that he had been assigned a contested property ownership case. The firm would be representing the property owner, the defendant, and if they prevailed the award would amount to several hundred thousand dollars, five percent of that amount going to the firm as its contingency fee. David would handle the case by himself, with one of the firm's four partners watching from the gallery.

David had been warned that this pressure-cooker method of testing young lawyers was standard practice. He had some research help from one of the firm's paralegals, but he was responsible for everything that happened. After a week of preparation, the trial began at ten o'clock on a Monday morning, King County Superior Court, Judge Marcia Hamilton presiding. The two parties had agreed that a jury would not be necessary; the decision would be Judge Hamilton's to make. She had already read the written briefs and the oral arguments should take no more than two hours.

Hamilton was one of the first women in Washington state to wear a black robe and she was known to be tough but fair. David knew this and had done his homework. He had anticipated each of her questions and his answers were persuasive. The whole thing was over within ninety minutes. The judge awarded the plaintiff two hundred and fifty thousand dollars and David had won his first case.

The law suit had drawn little attention in Seattle's newspapers and those in the gallery were mostly other lawyers, many of them young men and women who, like David, were new to the profession. A few senior partners from other firms did come but only because they had been asked to do so. Harvey Duncan knew these men well, most of them were his friends, and he wanted to know what they thought of this yearling, David McPherson. David knew nothing about this, of course, but within a week he was given another case, this one much more demanding. It would be held in the same court room but with a different judge and a twelve-person jury.

§

David won that case, too, but it wasn't easy.

His firm had decided to do a *pro bono* defense of a black man accused of grand larceny. According to the city's prosecuting attorney, he had broken into the home of an elderly widow who lived on Rainier Avenue, in one of the city's less affluent neighborhoods. The indictment stipulated it was 'an inside job,' that the thief knew the woman kept a large amount of cash in a shoebox under her bed, having learned this important detail from a mutual friend over drinks in a downtown bar. To make the case even more difficult for David, the man had served three months in the King County jail, having been found guilty of shop lifting at the downtown Macys department store.

His client, Cassius Downing, had been able to raise enough bail money to avoid jail but he was under strict orders not to leave the city before the case went to trial. When David talked to the man, he convincingly claimed to be innocent, saying it was a case of mistaken identity and that he could prove he wasn't even in Seattle at the time of the crime.

It was good experience for the young attorney. With Downing's help, David located two witnesses who were prepared to testify that they had been with Downing on an elk hunting trip, on the eastern slopes of the Cascade Mountains, some one hundred miles from the scene and on the same day of the alleged theft.

David drilled his witnesses over and over, to be sure they had their facts straight and would not contradict each other under cross-examination. 'And remember, you'll be under oath so stick to the story just as we've rehearsed it.'

On the day of the trial, when he walked into the court room, David was surprised to see a standing-room-only gallery: The *Seattle Post-Intelligencer* had run a front-page article, with Downing's picture, and all the details. The article included the gratuitous note that David McPherson, the *very young* defense attorney, was trying only his second case in a Seattle court room.

Included in the standing-room-only crowed were three principals from three other Seattle law firms. They had heard enough about this new lawyer and wanted to see for themselves: "Just how good IS this guy?"

The first to testify was the widow from Rainier Avenue, helped along by the city's prosecuting attorney. She hadn't actually seen the thief but after realizing that her life savings had been stolen, she reported the tragedy to the police. She told them she was sure that she heard a man's voice just before hearing her back door close, a man with a 'southern accent.' Then she looked over a collection of mug shots, all of them black, and she fingered Cassius Downing.

When it was David's turn, he guided his two witnesses through the much-rehearsed testimony. No problems there. But to make sure the jury understood the whole picture, he asked Downing if he had any *proof* that he had been elk hunting. Downing then handed David a brown, manila envelope and in the envelope were three one-day elk tags, issued by the Washington Department of Fish & Wildlife and a date/time-stamped receipt from a Shell gas station in Ellensburg, where Downing had topped off the tank of his pickup truck. David asked the judge that these items be entered into the evidential record and the judge then asked each juror to look at the contents of the envelope.

Thirty minutes later, the jury retired to the jury room to begin its deliberations. The judge gave them one hour for lunch and asked that they return a verdict as soon as possible. At two-thirty that same afternoon they returned to the court room and after the judge polled each juror, the jury foreman announced the obvious: Cassius Downing, not guilty.

The next morning, David found a note on his desk, inviting him to attend Harvey Duncan's weekly review, usually attended by only the senior partners and one secretary. It was a friendly meeting, with low-key congratulatory niceties coming from each of the partners. Just before David was dismissed, Duncan told him he would be receiving a fifteen percent increase in his salary and, if he kept up the good work, he could anticipate receiving a small percentage of the firm's net income. And, he could take the next three days off, to go fishing with his young wife.

That pattern repeated itself for, probably, the next twenty years. Law suits, court rooms, clients of every description, but always time for fishing with Cathy. The two of them had made an important decision, very early in their marriage: no kids. They agreed that their lifestyle, the pressures of work, being always on call, even some notoriety as David's courtroom successes became newsworthy—all of this was not the environment in which to raise children.

By the time David was in his middle fifties, he had become the junior partner and the firm had a slightly different name: Duncan, Winfield, James, Tolliver and McPherson. With that promotion came a sharp turn in his career: David was asked to represent his firm before the United States Ninth Circuit Court of Appeals, in San Francisco. This was now *federal* law, something relatively new to him, arguing issues of constitutional law, at the last level of jurisprudence before the Supreme Court in Washington, D.C.

This meant traveling from Seattle to San Francisco at least once every three months and whenever possible Cathy went with him. David's parents had passed away a few years earlier but he still thought of Portland as a kind of second home, and if he made up a sensible travel schedule, he and Cathy could re-acquaint themselves with Oregon's coastal rivers, those that flowed into the Pacific Ocean. Many of them had strong runs of steelhead trout and provided some of the best fly fishing on the West Coast.

On their very first trip south, David scheduled a stopover at the Nehalem River, a stream that flows into the ocean not far from Portland and one he had fished before. By now, both David and Cathy knew how to use the spey rod and they had a friendly competition going, who could make the longest casts? David could lay out at least sixty feet of ten-weight fly line, with Cathy not far behind. The were able to fish for only three hours but managed to catch and release one steelhead each, both fish fresh from the ocean and chrome-bright.

Those were wonderful years, as David later recalled. Working hard and having fun. But then, suddenly, the wonder turned to *wondering*. Why, why, why would Cathy fall victim to cancer? This beautiful, vibrant woman who even in her mid-sixties had the spunk and stamina of most women half her age.

The firm gave David as much time off as he needed to try to care for Cathy, in and out of Seattle's Swedish Hospital, weekly visits to her oncologist, chemo and radiation. None of it worked and within two months she was gone.

§

David held on for anther five years but he was a changed man. He knew it and so did his law partners. He gave his fly fishing gear—rods, reels, flies, everything—to the WFFC. Then he asked his law partners to release him from the firm and from there he would try to decide what to do with the rest of his life. As he later admitted, part of his problem was his anger with God: How could He possibly allow such a thing to happen? What had his beautiful Cathy done to deserve this?

After a week of grieving, David left Seattle and drove to Portland. Maybe that would help, going back to his roots. In Portland, he reconnected with the pastor who had led his parents' church. Pastor Dan remembered David, of course, and they met in his study for a long chat.

David told his story, admitting that he had no idea what to do next; without Cathy, his future was a huge, black hole.

For Pastor Dan, this was nothing new. He had lost count of the number of men and women who had experienced this kind of loss and grief. But he did have a few ideas. For example, what kind of community might David be looking for? Did he want to live in a *Christian* community or did that matter? Did he see himself as one who would be active in that community, or would he prefer a more passive life? Would he be comfortable living in a community made up of many widows and widowers, people much like himself? Did he want to live in Oregon, or did that matter?

David's responses to these thoughtful questions amounted to 'all of the above.' Yes, living in Oregon would be fine and, yes, living with others who are much like himself would probably be the best way to go. And, certainly, he would prefer to be surrounded by Christians.

Pastor Dan reached into his desk drawer and pulled out a brochure. 'Here, David, you should look at this. It might be the answer to your prayers.'

The multi-colored brochure was a product of the BeFriender ministry. David was vaguely aware of this, having heard of it while attending church services in Seattle. But the brochure was mostly about a Covenant Retirement Community located in Seaside, Oregon: Seaside Covenant Village. David read through its material and noticed that the village chaplain had included his phone number and email address.

'How far is it to Seaside?'

'Less than eighty miles, good highway, ninety minutes, at most.'

'Do you know this chaplain, Anthony Baker?'

'Oh, sure. I've known Tony for many years; he's one of the best. You'll like him. If you want to go now, I'll phone him and tell him you're coming.'

David hadn't been to Seaside in ages but he did remember the place as one of the most scenic parts of the Oregon coast. It had become a popular resort destination and it made sense that a retirement community would want to locate there. As he drove northwest toward Seaside he recalled that he and Cathy had been married by the chaplain at Seattle Pacific University and that SPU had close ties with the Covenant Church, that many of their graduates eventually became pastors or chaplains in the Covenant Church family.

David arrived in Seaside too late to visit chaplain Baker but he called him on his cell phone and asked to see him first thing the next morning. He found a motel, had dinner it its dining room and went to bed hoping that, God willing, his outlook on life was about to change.

§

Chaplain Anthony Baker was waiting for David. The day before, he'd talked about David with Pastor Dan and he knew what to expect. When David walked into his office he saw that David had a small notebook in his right hand, no doubt loaded with questions about Seaside Covenant Village.

The two men exchanged pleasantries over cups of hot coffee and then David went to his notebook. How many people live here? Are they all Christians? What kind of apartments are available? Do I need to be added to your waiting list? How much does it cost? Do you need a deposit now, or can I move right in? What about church services? How many widows live here? How many widowers, like me? And what about this BeFriender ministry? What's that all about?

Baker recalled that David had been a high-profile attorney and he felt as though he were being cross-examined in a court room. But he patiently answered David's questions, gave him a brochure that explained everything about Seaside Covenant, and another brochure that was devoted to the BeFriender ministry.

Pastor Dan was right. Chaplain Baker was 'one of the best,' and David found himself warming to the man. They talked for another twenty minutes and when David was about to leave Baker asked him a question he wasn't expecting.

'Have you heard of a lawyer, name of Bart Adamson? He's about your age and he clerked for one of the Supremes, Justice William Ashford, one of president Nixon's appointments.'

The question surprised David. Of course he knew *about* Adamson. Clerking for the Supreme Court was every lawyer's dream, but no, he'd never met the man. Why the question?

'Bart Adamson lives here. He came to Seaside Covenant right after he retired. And, like you, he's a native Oregonian and a widower, lost his wife three years ago. It may be only a coincidence, but he's also a fly fisherman. And he happens to be on our BeFriender team. I think you two should get together. I know you'd like each other and you certainly have a lot in common. But first, you need to decide if you want to join us. I'm sure you'd be a good fit but it's your decision.'

§

It was an easy decision. David walked directly from the chaplain's office to the village administration building, located the marketing office, explained his situation and wrote out a deposit check. His name was added to the waiting list and some time later he became a resident: Apartment 5321, Ocean View Drive, Seaside, Oregon, 97321.

David's arrival coincided with the monthly residents' council meeting and Bart Adamson was one of the first to meet him. That evening the two men had dinner together in the village dining room and, for each of them, a new friendship was born. Over dinner David recited the highlights of his career, mostly about his life with Cathy, some of his more interesting court room experiences. He told Bart it was no secret that he was still in deep grief over Cathy's death, that he was angry with God for allowing it to happen and that until he could shed these feelings of anger and resentment he wouldn't be very good company.

Over the next six months the two men got together at least once each week. Bart mostly listened to David's laments but while doing so he would occasionally offer a passage of scripture that was relevant to the issue. And at the end of each visit the two men prayed together, asking God for solutions. Bart had explained to David the BeFriender 'rules' about confidentiality, assuring him that whatever they talked about would never be repeated.

§

Then it happened. David awoke early one morning with the feeling that something was much different. He'd been dreaming about Cathy when suddenly the dream was interrupted by a voice that had to be Cathy's. She assured him that she was just fine, that everything in Heaven was just as they thought it would be and that he could be confident that one day he would join her. 'There are no tears here, David. Please believe that.'

After breakfast, David phoned his BeFriender, Bart. He told him about his dream and asked him if he'd like to join him in a joyous celebration. Perhaps it wasn't the most appropriate thing to say, but he couldn't help himself.

'Let's go fishing,' he said.

CHAPTER 8

Billy

§

May 25, 1937, Caddo County, Oklahoma

THE KEROSENE LAMP AT HIS beside had gone dark hours ago and when
it did, Billy fell asleep almost at once. He had been reading the last
few verses of St. Paul's letter to Timothy, the second one, and that always made him sad because he knew Paul would be martyred within a
few months. His Sunday school teacher had asked all the kids to come
prepared to talk about Timothy: What did they know about him, why
was a much younger man such a favorite of the about-to-die evangelist?
Would Timothy be able to do the things that Paul had asked of him?
Billy had asked his parents about that, just hours ago at the dinner table.
Billy's father always had answers for his son's questions but this time he
let his wife do the talking.

Billy's mother, Sarah, also taught Sunday school but her students were
older, nine through twelve. And, at the time, they were working their way
through the Psalms. Each student was assigned a psalm to memorize and
then recite it, from memory, in front of the other kids. It was good practice, 'stretching their minds,' as Billy later recalled.

It was the wind that awakened him. One of the windows shattered,
shards of glass flying in all directions and his bedroom, within seconds,
was covered with prairie dust. The roof was shaking so loudly that it

awakened the whole family. Billy, his mother and father, and his sister, Rebecca, ran to the storm shelter, just a few steps beyond the back door. The shelter had been constructed to resist the occasional tornado that came through this part of Oklahoma, but when the winds howled, as they often did these days, the shelter was their only refuge.

They waited until nearly dawn, testing the cellar door to be sure it was safe to go outside. Their home was still on the waiting list for electricity, and as long as kerosene was available they should be okay. But in the poorly-ventilated storm cellar, the smell of burning kerosene was very unpleasant.

The Mason family, on their farm about a mile to the east, had electricity. They had waited nearly two years for president Roosevelt's new program—the Rural Electrification Act—to bring that so-called 'magic light' to their home. Even the out-buildings had light. The nearest hardware store, about fifteen miles to the north in Apache, was busy stocking shelves with this new 'stuff,' electric light bulbs, wiring, switches, sockets and other things that very few people understood.

The wind finally subsided enough that it was safe to leave the shelter and the family moved back into its home. Billy had been through this before and he and his sister were expected to sweep up as much prairie dust as possible, dump it outside and then help their mother prepare breakfast. Billy's father had stepped outside to see what he could of the alfalfa fields. Their home had been built on a slight rise, roughly in the center of their eighty-acre spread, nearly all of it planted in alfalfa, and with his eight-power binoculars he could see well enough.

In good times, before Billy was born, the alfalfa harvest had supported the family quite well and Billy's father was able to buy a used tractor and sell the two horses that had been pulling the harvester for the past five years. But now the weather had changed and the heavy winds were a constant. One of the Oklahoma City newspapers had already referred to the region as The Dust Bowl, a name that fit perfectly.

Billy's father stepped back into the kitchen, not saying a word, and seated himself at the breakfast table. The others joined him in prayer and after giving thanks for their meal he told them what they had feared for many weeks.

'I'm sorry to have to tell you this, but we're not going to make it. Most of that crop will never mature, not enough moisture, and that wind storm last night was the last straw. I'll drive up to Apache later today and see if I can persuade the bank to assume the mortgage on the property. Then we'll have to move on. We all know the Jensen family moved, somewhere in California, I think it was, yes, to the Imperial Valley. I received a letter from Hank Jensen and he said the farming there is a lot better than it was here. He was able to lease fifty acres of soy beans and because they can grow two crops every year, he's doing pretty well.'

§

Billy's father, Harry Blackwell, had driven the seven miles to Apache many times. It was a small town, fewer than a thousand people, and its only church, The Apache Southern Baptist Center, had been the family's place of worship for many years. Just as important, the town was home to those stores and shops the entire region depended on: groceries, hardware, a Texaco gas station, feed and fertilizer, a blacksmith, a one-room school house, a two-chair barber shop and, of course, the First State Bank of Oklahoma.

The bank's manager, a good friend of Harry Blackwell, knew the entire region was in trouble. Some of the dust storms had darkened the sky all the way to the east coast. One report estimated that, on average, four inches of precious top soil had disappeared and if that weren't bad enough, rainfall was about one-half of what it had been six or seven years earlier.

Harry Blackwell knew as well as anyone that the bank had been instructed by its owners in Oklahoma City to buy up these mortgages, and pay a decent price for them. They were taking the long view, calculating that, sooner or later, the weather would change for the better and when it did, the bank would own all those properties, sell them to new owners and make a tidy profit. Well, that 'long view' didn't do the Blackwell family any good and like a lot of other folks whose farms were spread all over Caddo County, they had to move on, mostly west to California.

§

What to take with them? After a week of heckling, Harry Blackwell had been able to trade his John Deere tractor for a 1936 Ford flat-bed truck. When fitted with four-foot sideboards, the truck could haul most of the family possessions. They had two cats and a dog and a nearby neighbor had agreed to take them in. Harry would drive the truck and Sarah could drive the 1934 Chevy four-door. He calculated that at a distance of 1,200 miles, and perhaps as many as 150 miles a day, they should reach the Imperial Valley in no more than eight days.

§

June 6, 1937, Imperial County, California

Five flat tires later, the Blackwell 'caravan' limped into Heber, California, a village of fewer than a thousand people. When he left home, Harry knew no more about the Imperial Valley than what Hank Jensen had told him in a letter. Hank's farm was somewhere near Heber, a community that had been established by the Imperial Land Company in an effort to encourage people to come to the region and farm the fertile land.

He drove into a Texaco gas station and asked the operator if he knew Hank Jenson.

'Sure, I know Hank. He's one of my better customers. Why do you ask?'

'Hank had a farm, not far from mine, in Oklahoma. We were neighbors and good friends, He asked me to look him up if I ever decided to move west. Well, we're here now and I'd like to find him.'

'Oh, that's it! Yeah, sure. We call you folks *Okies*. Do you know that? We know why you're here. You can't make it back home, so you come to California and try to do your faming here. Do you know that every time you do that, you put a bunch of our people out of work? Hell, there's a depression going on, in case you didn't know. President Roosevelt said so. And he was right. A lot of our people are out of work, looking for any kind of job they can find. Then you *Okies* show up and - - -'

'Okay, okay. I get the message. Just tell me how to find Hank. I'll fill up and leave.'

§

Grudgingly, the Texaco man wrote out Jenson's phone number. If he refused, it would cost him another customer and that he could ill afford. Harry made the call from the station's hand-crank telephone and after waiting six rings, Hilda Jensen answered. She insisted that Harry and his family spend the night with them, then explained how to find their farm, only three miles from the gas station.

It was old home week for the two families. They enjoyed a huge meal together and after doing the dishes they talked long into the night. Hank thought of himself as an old hand at Imperial Valley farming and he had some useful suggestions to help Harry get started.

First thing. You visit the local office of the Imperial Land Company and tell them why you're here and what you'd like to do. They have parcels of land that they'll let you farm, up to 160 acres. They'll take twenty percent of whatever you make on selling your crops and you can do this as long as you wish. Eventually, if you can afford it, you can buy the land then you're on your own.

And because they want to attract more people—not just from Oklahoma, but from other states, too—they'll help you arrange a mortgage with the bank so you can begin building a house and the necessary out-buildings. This is a good deal and they know the word will spread.

Best of all, the guys who run this operation—some of them are from Oklahoma, just like we are—are sick and tired of all the prejudice they see being thrown at us: us *Okies*. It's even worse than the insults they hurl at those Mexicans who have the courage to come up here and look for work.

And one more thing. I don't know why but there are no Southern Baptist churches in this neck of the woods. Hilda and I finally decided to worship at the local Lutheran church. They accept anyone, so long as they believe. In fact, they'll even baptize children who were born into Southern Baptist families. The other churches around here—they turn up their noses at anyone who wasn't born in California. That's a sad thing but it's the truth.

§

October 10, 1957, near El Centro, California

Twenty years later Billy Blackwell owned his own farm, free and clear. It was a huge spread, adjacent to the acres upon acres of citrus—oranges, lemons, limes—that had long since made his father a wealthy man.

Billy had gone to school at the California Institute of Agronomy, in San Diego, and specialized in soil management and crop selection. His memories of those Oklahoma dust storms had taught him a lesson: Select your crops wisely and take care of the soil in which they grow. He now owned more than 160 acres and he knew that diversification was the key to good management. In the Imperial Valley, a good farmer could grow just about anything, and Billy had chosen mostly vegetables, knowing that he could grow at least two crops each year and the rapidly-expanding California market would buy everything he had to sell.

Carrots, sweet corn, chili peppers, onions and melons. Those were his favorites. But he also planted many acres in alfalfa, the very same crop that had failed in those long-ago Oklahoma dust storms.

On the advice of his attorney, Billy had incorporated himself, naming his business *Blackwell, Inc.* That decision had made a difference, owing to the way the California Business and Occupation tax code had been structured by the legislature in Sacramento. It also helped with his advertizing, as he wanted to attract and maintain a reliable work force, made up mostly of immigrants from Mexico.

From Billy's perspective, that work force was the key to success. He needed a reliable foreman to make his plan work and after interviewing several candidates he settled on Miguel Martinez, a bi-lingual 30-year old who had migrated from Juarez to El Centro. Billy recounted for Miguel his experiences as a younger man, when he was struggling with his reputation as an interloper, a low-life *Okie*, someone who could not be trusted.

Billy told Miguel that his company had a zero-tolerance policy toward any kind of discrimination and it was Miguel's responsibility to enforce it. Billy told Miguel that if he ever had any doubts about his responsibilities, he could ask himself 'What would Jesus do?'

Further, it would be up to Miguel to select workers from the many applicants, to treat them fairly—especially the women—and to make certain they were satisfied with their housing. If they wanted to worship on Sundays, the company had its own bus and would take them to and from a Catholic church in El Centro where the two priests spoke both English and Spanish. That same bus was to be used during the week to transport the children to and from school.

After Miguel had been on the job for six months, Billy could see that the man could run the farm almost as well as he could. That left Billy with more time for his family. He had married a young woman who grew up in Bakersfield, California and it bothered her not at all that Billy was from Oklahoma. Juliana Peterson was her name, 'Julie' to her friends. She had studied nursing at the Bakersfield community college and she was active in her Baptist church. While they were still dating, Billy learned that not all Baptists are the same. There were no Southern Baptist churches in the region but after worshipping with Julie he saw little difference in what he had known at home in Oklahoma.

Soon after the wedding, Billy gave his bride a tour of the *Blackwell, Inc.* holdings: the crops, the out buildings and the workers' living quarters. Billy's field crews had grown to twenty adults, some with children. The California state health inspectors visited the living quarters every six months and Blackwell, Inc. had yet to receive a 'Notice of Insufficiencies.' Julie thought that was a good beginning but she asked her husband what happens if someone is injured or becomes ill? Why not set up a small clinic right here, on the property? Julie's nursing training had qualified her to work in such a clinic and her Spanish was good enough that she could help, especially with the children. Her *real* motive was to share the love of Jesus with anyone who visited the clinic.

§

Within a year, the clinic became the most talked-about facility of its kind in all of Imperial County. Instead of going into El Centro for routine medical checkups, Blackwell Inc's workers used the clinic and it wasn't long before workers from other farms were coming for treatment. Billy and Julie decided they wouldn't turn anyone away, so long as the workload was manageable, but Julie soon found it necessary to hire an assistant. She was a Mexican woman who had a nurses' certificate and who worshipped at the same Catholic church in El Centro as most of the workers.

Word of the clinic's popularity and success eventually reached into the offices of El Centro's leading newspaper, *The Imperial Valley News*, and a front-page article appeared, with photographs of Billy, Julie, Miguel and several of the workers. The article was written by a Christian reporter who underscored the *spiritual* dimension that was so apparent to anyone visiting the clinic. There were take-home Spanish-language bibles in the waiting room and several Warner Sallman paintings of Jesus on the office walls.

The clinic soon discovered it had another, unexpected, problem. As the word spread, Miguel found himself inundated with requests for employment, far more than he could handle and about two times the number of workers needed to plant, cultivate and harvest the crops. Billy decided the company should maintain a waiting list, with addresses and phone numbers of the applicants. That should ensure a continuity in his workforce that would guarantee stability far into the future.

§

That stability gave Billy time to pursue other interests. He had been invited to join El Centro's Rotary club. The club met for lunch every Tuesday and always had a good program, usually a speaker who had something interesting to say. Billy's sponsor, Paul Anderson, had visited Billy's farm several times. He wasn't a competitor because he grew only grain crops, wheat, barley and several acres of potatoes. Like Billy, he was a committed Christian and a member of Billy's Baptist church. Anderson told Billy that the upcoming program would feature state senator Fred Mitchell.

On their way to the meeting, Anderson told Billy that he had been writing letters to Mitchell, in which he complained about Mexican farm workers who had entered the United States illegally. They were being hired by some of the valley's citrus growers who were looking for workers who were willing to work for below-scale wages. Anderson worried that sooner or later, more farmers would follow suit and if that happened those workers who had entered the country legally would have reason to complain, fearing that their wage scale was being threatened. The two talked about this and by the time they arrived at the meeting they decided to discuss the issue with Senator Mitchell, following his presentation.

And talk they did, for more than thirty minutes. It was the first time Billy had ever spoken with an elected official. Mitchell was likeable, courteous and well-versed on the issues. And then Mitchell surprised Billy when he told him that he had heard about Billy and his farm and its clinic, about his cordial relationship with his Mexican workers. It seemed to Mitchell, he said, that Billy should consider going into politics. There happened to be a vacancy on the El Central city council, as yet unfilled. If Mitchell were to put in a good word, Billy could fill the vacancy as an interim appointment. It would give him a year at hands-on politics, without having to run his own campaign. At the end of the year he could decide what to do next.

Billy thanked the senator and told him this was a decision he didn't want to make by himself. He'd talk to his wife about it and then let him know.

§

Julie's response to her husband's news was more than enthusiastic. She had always thought that Billy was smart and determined enough to be more than a successful farmer. And she could help. For the next four weeks the two of them drove into El Centro three times a week. They devoured every book they could find in the city's library that had anything to do with the city, the Imperial Valley, its history, its leading personalities and, of course, its politics.

The city council met once a week, Wednesday morning from ten to noon. The city manager, a woman in her late fifties, was a no-nonsense administrator who knew her job and expected the council members to know theirs. She took an immediate liking to Billie who seemed to know as much about the issues as did the old-timers. After the third meeting she told Billy to consider himself the go-to councilman on issues having to do with the region's agriculture. It was a big job, she told him, but she was certain he could handle it.

§

At the end of Billy's one-year interim appointment his council colleagues urged him to run for a full two-year term. He was making a difference, especially with regard to county ordinances that affected agricultural workers' safety and health. Although Billy never spoke of it, they knew he would pray, silently, when it was time to vote on the more contentious issues. Although he was flattered by their expressions of confidence, Billy decided that he'd better go back to full-time farming. There were others who could run for office and do just as well. And although Julie was disappointed, she had to agree that it was the right decision.

Then, not long after Billy's return to full-time farming, something happened that both puzzled and frightened him. One evening, following their evening meal, they were helping each other with the dishes when Julie suddenly turned to him and with anger in her voice said, 'I don't like the way you've been treating me.' Jimmy, startled and at a loss for words, mumbled something like 'I'm sorry, Sweetheart. You know I would never hurt you. What *is* it?' Julie, pouting: 'Well, if you don't know I'm not going to tell you. You'll just have to figure it out for yourself!'

A few moments later, it was as though nothing had happened. They finished the dishes, watched television for an hour and went to bed. Billy lay awake, silently asking God to help him. Something was terribly wrong and he had no idea what it might be.

The next morning, at the breakfast table, Billy noticed that Julie had put out two butter knives at each place setting, but no other silverware. After they were seated, Billy reached for the coffee carafe and Julie said, 'Oh, you can't do that. We need *spoons*.' Billy: 'That's okay, Honey, I'll get them.'

Then he knew. His precious Juliana was showing the very early symptoms of dementia, something that always happens 'to someone else.'
Billy asked himself, 'Does *she* realize what's happening?' Answer, 'Probably not.'

After breakfast, Billy walked over to Julie's clinic and found a reference book that discussed dementia. What he read was not encouraging: The symptoms almost always become progressively more pronounced but the rate at which this happens varies widely from one person to another. Thus far, there is no known cure. A visit to a neurologist can be helpful because standardized testing can reveal the severity of the condition. In many cases, the affected person does not realize— or refuses to acknowledge—that he/she *is* affected. Worse, in many circumstances the entire family chooses to live in a state of denial, as though nothing has changed.

The reference book's final paragraph suggested that as more and more is becoming understood about dementia, hospitals and retirement homes are developing skilled nursing facilities with specially-trained personnel. It listed a telephone number in Sacramento that would lead to more information.

A week after placing the call to the state capital, Billy received a list of facilities in California that were licensed to accept patients with cognitive loss. He realized that his life was about to change, that if Julie were to receive the care she needed, his Imperial Valley farm was not the place. He knew he could sell the farm; he'd received inquiries from prospective buyers but how would he explain to Julie why they were moving? And moving to – where?

To his surprise, it was his foreman Miguel who provided the answer. Miguel had noticed the changes in Julie and he asked Billy about them. Then Miguel suggested that Julie speak with Miguel's wife. His mother-in-law was dealing with dementia, the symptoms were similar and perhaps the two women could compare notes. The goal was to help Julie understand what was happening; assuming that bridge could be crossed, everything else would become much easier.

And that is what happened. Within minutes after her long conversation with Miguel's wife, Julie returned from the clinic and sat down beside her husband. 'Billy, now I know what's wrong. And it's only going to get worse. But, now that I know, I'm going to do my best to be the wife you've always known. I trust you, I love you, and I'll do whatever you say.'

§

Then the search began. Someone at their church had suggested to Billy that he might be interested in a Covenant Retirement Communities facility. That would be a place where he could be certain of a Christian environment and many of them included special facilities for residents who were dealing with memory loss.

Neither of them had ever seen the Pacific Ocean and San Diego seemed like a good place to begin looking. The El Centro library included a reference room that featured brochures from all over the United States. Most of these were for tourists but a few of them were intended for people who were looking for a new place to live.

And, sure enough, there it was, in red, white, and blue: A brochure published by the Ocean Beach Covenant Village. A quick glance at the small map showed it to be a suburb of San Diego. Perfect.

April 30, 2004, San Diego, California

Six months after selling their farm, Billie and Julie moved into Ocean Beach Covenant. They told the marketing office that after living as 'flat-landers' for a lifetime, it would be nice to have a good view of the Pacific Ocean. They chose a two-bedroom apartment on the fifth floor, the living room window facing due West.

At nine o'clock in the morning of Day Two, Billy walked over to the chaplain's office and introduced himself. Chaplain Mary McGovern had been in the Covenant Church family all of her adult life. Now in her mid-sixties, she was thinking about retiring but she was the most popular and well-known person on the campus and some of her neighbors had virtually dared her to retire: 'We *need* you!'

Billy took his time explaining to Mary as much as he could about his wife's condition. After listening, she told him that Julie was not alone, there were as many as fifteen others who were dealing with similar issues. When the dementia had advanced to the point that Julie could no longer share the apartment with Billy, she could move to the unit that specialized in caring for residents with memory loss. It was known as *Reflections* and there were at least two specially-trained care givers on duty, 24/7. Julie would take her meals with the others in their private dining room. She would have her own bedroom and bathroom and share the living room and library with the other residents. She could attend Sunday worship services with everyone else. The village employed a full-time activities director who saw to it that there was something interesting, sometimes even challenging, to do every day.

Before leaving Mary McGovern's office, Billy decided to tell her what was *really* bothering him, in addition to Julie's condition. He had become very angry, angry with God for allowing this to happen to his wife; a wife who had been totally loyal to him from Day One, a wife who loved and cared for people, people of whatever color or background, a wife who had been a devoted Christian her entire life. Did Chaplain Mary have any suggestions for how Billy might deal with this? He had prayed about it, many times, but his anger was getting worse and that frightened him.

'Billy, please, read this. It's a brochure that describes our BeFriender ministry. After you've looked it over and prayed about it, come back and see me. I know I can help.'

Chaplain Mary's 'help' was Harry Smithers, a retired wheat and barley farmer from Iowa. Harry and his wife had moved to Ocean Beach village shortly after selling their farm and Chaplain Mary, after getting to know the man, decided he'd make a good candidate for BeFriender training. Now in his fifth year in the program, he had befriended three men, each of them a retired farmer and the results of his ministry had been very good. Smithers was a rather quiet man but a good listener and most people liked him as soon as they met him. It helped that he and his wife had been in the Covenant church family since they were teenagers.

Mary asked the two men to join her in the campus lunch room, a good way, she thought, to introduce them to each other and at the same time talk about why she thought a BeFriender relationship with Harry Smithers would be a good thing for Billy Blackwell. Like most chaplains, Mary was a good judge of character and the two men warmed to each other immediately. Before leaving, they agreed to meet in Billy's apartment at ten o'clock the following morning.

That first visit took most of an hour. Harry explained to Billy some of the BeFriender ministry's history, pointing out that every campus in the CRC system had its own group of trained BeFrienders, each of them in supervision with the campus chaplain. He assured Billy that whatever he had to say would go no further, that confidentiality was one of the cornerstones of the ministry. If Billy wished, the two men could pray together about whatever they wished, knowing that God was present and He would hear their prayers.

§

As often happens, Harry and Billy became close friends. They visited every week, Harry mostly listening, patiently letting Billy express his anger and frustration. When Billy asked a question, Harry often responded by quoting an appropriate passage of scripture. The process took nearly a year but, eventually, Billy had come to terms with Julie's illness. He was certain that the Apostle Paul was right: *And we know that God causes all things to work together for good to those who love God, to those who are called according to His purpose.*

His beloved Julie would not get better, but that no longer mattered. They had shared a good life and an abiding faith in a personal, loving God. They were living together in a good place, secure in the knowledge that their health needs would be met. And they had the hope of eternal life, together with their Lord.

CHAPTER 9

Roger

§

Seven A.M., May 5, 1949, University of Washington, lower campus

THE CONIBEAR SHELLHOUSE WAS EMPTY but the entryway was unlocked, as Roger Longworth knew it would be. He had arrived early, knowing that Coach Murphy would expect everyone to be ready to go in less than an hour. It was Thursday and the California crew would be arriving the next day. Yesterday's time trials for the varsity eight—five minutes and forty-six seconds—had been disappointing and Murphy was determined to make the boat go faster. Roger thought he might be moved from bow to the second or third seat. He could do that if asked; he'd rowed all the seats except stroke.

The Saturday race was to be the usual two thousand meters, through the Montlake Cut to the finish line beyond. Saturday would be Opening Day in Seattle, with participating crews from Vancouver, B.C., one all the way from New Zealand, then Stanford and USC. But it was the California crew that was the big threat. The year before, the Huskies had rowed against Cal and they lost, but by less than a boat length. That was on Cal's home waters at Redwood Shores. This time would be different. It had been three years since the Huskies had been beaten on Lake Washington, and that by the Yale crew, at the time the best in the United States.

But, win or lose, Roger knew that Debbie McCabe would be waiting, just outside the shell house. From there, they'd go to Sparky's Pizza Palace on the Ave and talk about their future. Both of them were graduating in June and the wedding would take place six weeks later, in Debbie's sorority house.

It was a perfect day; clear skies and a three mph quartering wind. Cal got off to an early lead with the Kiwis right alongside, the Husky shell about a half-length back, with USC and Stanford two lengths back but keeping pace. At the thousand meter mark the Husky coxswain called for their second big ten and the boat slowly moved ahead, white-tipped oars flashing in the sunlight. They crossed the finish line with a half boat-length of open water between Cal and New Zealand. It wasn't record time, but close: 5:44.6.

Back at the shell house, the eight oarsmen performed the obligatory rite of heaving their coxswain into Lake Washington's still-chilly waters. Only winners do this, and the Husky coxswain, all 140 pounds of him, couldn't have been happier. It was his third dunking of the season and there would be three more races, the last in late June when the Huskies would compete in the IRA regatta on Mercer Lake in New Jersey.

After a hot shower and a change of clothes, Roger met Debbie in front of the shell house. Teasing, she asked him if he had enough energy to walk to Sparky's. He reminded her that even though he had been driving his body to its extreme limit for nearly six minutes, any in-shape oarsman's heart and other bodily functions return to normal within thirty minutes. Their daily practice sessions often go on for an hour or more—so, Debbie, not to worry.

They found their favorite table, at the back of the room, and ordered two eight-inch pizzas, a small green salad and two glasses of Rainier beer. Strictly speaking, beer wasn't on the 'approved' list for Washington's oarsmen but Roger allowed himself this one treat whenever they had just won a big race.

As they both knew would happen, the conversation quickly turned to their upcoming wedding. Debbie had been attending University Presbyterian church. She rarely missed a Sunday but she could never persuade Roger to come with her. He claimed to be 'agnostic' and that was probably true. Roger's parents had not been church-goers and so he and his sister never saw the inside of a church. The only bible he'd ever seen was one kept in the library of his Chi Psi fraternity house. That's how he'd met Debbie. She was a Sigma Kappa, and her sorority house was right next door.

They had discussed this more than once—*where* to have the wedding. Roger had told her he'd feel like a hypocrite if the wedding were held in a church. Debbie finally decided to do it in her sorority house. She loved Roger enough to overlook his agnosticism and they tried to avoid talking about it. Roger willingly agreed that Debbie should ask the pastor of her church to do the wedding. Presbyterian, Methodist, Baptist; it made no difference to him.

§

The Husky varsity eight went on to set a school record. It won all of its remaining races, finishing the season with a convincing win at the IRA meet on Mercer Lake, a two boat length win over the Yale shell. The trip back to Seattle, aboard the Great Northern Railway's *Empire Builder,* gave the boys three days to celebrate, relax and talk about their futures. Most would graduate as soon as they returned.

Roger had already applied and been accepted for one year of graduate school. He had done well in his physics and chemistry classes and he knew that all high schools taught those subjects. He could start out as an interim science/math teacher and work his way up. He knew that such a career would never make him a wealthy man. He also knew—and it was a selfish thought, he had to admit to himself—that Debbie's parents were well off and that some day she would inherit their estate.

They were married on Saturday, June 25, at three in the afternoon. It was a simple ceremony, mostly fraternity brothers and sorority sisters there to wish them well. Roger's parents were on a business trip to Honolulu, something they couldn't postpone or cancel. Debbie's parents were there and her closest friend and roommate served as her bridesmaid. Roger chose the president of the Chi Psi house as his best man. Much to Roger's surprise, all seven of his crew mates appeared, each one insisting on kissing the bride at the conclusion of the service.

Following the reception, the newlyweds drove to the Roosevelt Hotel in downtown Seattle. The next morning they would take the ferry across Puget Sound to the McCabe summer home on Bainbridge Island, Debbie's wedding gift from her parents. They told her she could stay as long as she liked. Later in the summer, she would be going back to the university's School of Nursing. Her four years of pre-med studies had not been wasted and she had a 3.4 GPA to prove it.

That summer of 1949 passed all too quickly. They had moved into a low-rent boarding house, four blocks west of the campus, and were able to walk to their part-time jobs. Debbie found work at the university book store and Roger signed on as an assistant crew coach. He worked mostly with freshmen and sophomores, and some of them, he thought, would eventually be able to carry on the Husky winning tradition.

Fast-forward now to the summer of 1950. Roger's search for full-time employment had come up empty. He soon learned that science teachers in the Pacific Northwest were a dime a dozen. Not so with Debbie. She could find a job as a nurse nearly anywhere she chose to apply. But Roger was the breadwinner and he needed to find work. As Roger thought about it later, if you can't be good it helps to be lucky.

Debbie's married sister had been living in Colorado Springs for the past three years and, like her sister, she was smart and kept herself informed of the local scene. After several phone calls, she told Debbie that Roger should be able to get a job as a math/science teacher at College America. The school's curriculum focused on health services but every student was required to take at least one course in one of the hard sciences.

Debbie's sister suggested she continue her nursing program. There were three hospitals in Colorado Springs and they were always in need of women with nursing skills. That meant that each of them should be able to find worthwhile employment, both of them along their preferred career paths.

Before the summer was over they had exchanged many letters and even a few expensive long-distance phone calls. Debbie knew that her hyper-active sister was helping at her end and by the beginning of September Roger had secured a position as a math/science instructor at College America and Debbie as a nurse's aide in Colorado Springs' St. Francis Medical Center.

The move to Colorado Springs obliged Roger to borrow a pick-up truck from his new father-in-law. The newlyweds had very little furniture to move but they did not want to take the overly-long trip by rail and flying was out of the question. United Air Lines had recently established a route between Seattle and Denver, using a propeller-driven Douglass DC-6, with a maximum ceiling of 10,000 feet. But the word was already out that flying in that airplane over two mountain ranges—the Cascades and the Rocky Mountains—could be a very unsettling experience.

Along with the pick-up truck came an interest-free loan, just enough to help Roger and Debbie find an apartment, somewhere close to their jobs. They chose a two-floor walk-up on the western edge of the city which, oddly enough, provided a breathtaking, long-range view the Broadmoor Hotel and Country Club, with its golf course, swimming pools, polo grounds and two-hundred-dollars-per-night rooms.

§

Roger's new job at College America was everything he could have hoped for. The faculty members were mostly young men and women, the college president only forty-five years old. With his engaging personality, Roger quickly became one of the group, easily making new friends. It was obvious to him that his prowess as an oarsman didn't impress anyone on the faculty; they paid no attention to rowing and because rowing events were never on television they knew next to nothing about it.

Fishing, hunting and skiing were another matter; three activities about which Roger knew next to nothing. A few days after his arrival he decided to forego Debbie's brown-bag lunch, telling her he wanted to try something different. Many of the faculty took their mid-day meal in the college cafeteria and he'd heard the food was pretty good. He had chatted briefly with one of the math teachers who mentioned something about the fly fishing season improving, now that Fall had finally come to the Rocky Mountains. *Fly fishing?* He had a vague idea about what that meant. In fact, his friend who had rowed the number four seat used to go fly fishing in August, somewhere in the Cascade Mountains, near Mr. Rainier. He caught rainbow trout, he said, and brought them back to his fraternity house so the cook could prepare them for breakfast the next morning.

Roger's new math teacher friend, Bob Summerville, invited Roger and Debbie to come with him the next time he went fishing. That would be next Saturday and they would drive west to the North Fork of the South Platte River, probably the most beautiful trout stream in all of Colorado. It would be an all-day trip, with some modest hiking required to get to the best parts of the river. Bob had done this many times and he thought he knew where they could find both rainbow and brown trout. Perhaps Debbie could prepare box lunches for the three of them. Should be fun.

It *was* fun. They returned to Colorado Springs late Saturday evening, with three sixteen-inch rainbow trout carefully wrapped in moist burlap and stowed in the cool darkness of the car's trunk. Roger had been intrigued by Bob's casting technique. He seemed to be able to drop his fly exactly where he wanted it and if a fish was within sight of the fly he invariably hooked it. He was using barbless hooks and released three smaller fish, unharmed, into the river's icy-cold waters. On the drive home, Debbie asked her husband if he thought he would like to learn how. Roger said he wasn't so sure. He didn't want to leave Debbie at home while he went fishing and if they both took lessons, it would probably cost too much: fly rods, reels, line, fishing vests, waders, flies, and a bunch of other stuff.

Maybe deer hunting would be the better way to go. A rifle, a few shells and some good hiking boots and he'd be all set. The deer season was almost upon them, opening in mid-November. Roger thought he could make one trip, without Debbie, just to learn if he could handle it. He'd never fired a rifle but there was a shooting range west of the city and he could practice there. He would not go hunting alone, but he thought Bob might come along, or perhaps another one of the men he was getting to know at the college.

§

Roger visited the shooting range twice, each time working with the range's instructor. At the end of his second visit he was able to put his 30.06 caliber bullet within two inches of the one-inch bulls-eye, one hundred yards distant. His instructor told him that very few people are able to do that and he assumed it was Roger's experience as a Husky oarsman that made the difference: precision, timing, and steady nerves.

After waiting for the season to open in mid-November, Bob invited Roger to go with him. They drove west to the Sawatch Range in the White River National Forest, found a camp ground and spent the night in Bob's pick-up camper. Roger had never before slept in a sleeping bag, but with the overnight temperature dipping to near-freezing, he was pleasantly surprised that he stayed warm and comfortable enough for a good night's rest.

They awoke early, just after sunrise, and around a small campfire Bob answered Roger's unspoken question: 'What about breakfast?' A heavy, cast-iron and blackened skillet, two tablespoons of olive oil, four scrambled eggs and two slices of ham, along with two sides of toast; plus a pot of hot, black coffee; that was the answer to Roger's question. While Bob cleaned up, Roger prepared a sack lunch: peanut butter sandwiches, Snicker bars, two bananas and bottled water.

Bob had been through this routine many times and he assumed Roger was still in good enough shape to endure the several miles of uphill hiking that would be required if they were to find deer. These Rocky Mountain Whitetail deer preferred to browse on lichens and ferns, usually found about eight thousand feet above sea level. In the morning hours the cooler air mass slides downhill, pushing their scent away from the deer but they also needed to be as quiet as possible. If they were lucky they might be able to get off one shot; more than one, unlikely.

Each of their Springfield 30.06 rifles was fitted with a telescopic scope, which they had sighted in a week earlier at the same shooting range. Bob told Roger to use 150 yards as the 'spot-on' setting. A shot at more than 250 yards would be too risky and the last thing they wanted was a wounded animal that they could never find.

The two men walked, sometimes crawled, most of the day. With his eight-power binoculars Bob finally spotted four deer, slowly climbing toward the top of a distant ridge, but they were at least a thousand yards away, on the far side of a deep, boulder-strewn ravine. No good.

By late afternoon they decided to call it quits. It would be nearly an hour's walk back to camp and then the long drive to Colorado Springs.

§

The next morning, a Sunday, Roger found himself in their small kitchen, preparing breakfast for himself and Debbie. It was a routine he didn't much like because she would be going to church while he stayed at home with nothing much to do except read the Sunday edition of the *Denver Post*. He'd thought about subscribing to one of the two Seattle newspapers but that was an expense they couldn't afford. And, if he was honest about it, he felt guilty about seeing his wife going off to church while he stayed home.

Remembering Bob's campfire breakfast, Roger thought he could improve on that by adding some hash-brown potatoes. He had watched the cooks at the Chi Psi house do this and it seemed simple enough. And it was. Debbie complimented him at the breakfast table, then off to church. On her way out the back door: 'I left you a note on the coffee table, Sweetheart. You might want to read it. See you in a couple of hours.'

He noticed that Debbie had purchased a second bible which she had left on their living-room coffee table, something he couldn't miss seeing. She hadn't said anything about it but she didn't need to. She hoped he'd read it, or at least look at a few pages. And maybe, just maybe, he'd do that—after she left for church. He could breeze through the *Denver Post* sports pages, then take a look at Debbie's bible. Or, was it intended to be *his* bible?

§

After putting the breakfast dishes into the dishwasher, Roger walked into the living room, sat down beside the coffee table. The bible was lying there with Debbie's note attached:

My beloved: It's not easy for us to talk about these things but this note will tell you what's on my heart. I love you, Roger, and I want to spend the rest of my life with you. What I want more than anything right now is for you to know how I feel about my Christian faith and why I feel that way. And I pray that, some day, you'll feel the same way.

When you came home yesterday from your hunting trip with Bob, you raved about the beauty of your surroundings in the mountains: the trees, the streams, the glaciers, the wildlife. You should ask yourself, Sweetheart, did all that just 'happen' or is it possible that a higher being is responsible? The bible tells us that God created all this beauty and that He did it for each of us to enjoy. And Saint Paul, in his letter to the church at Rome, goes even further: He writes that anyone who can see all that beauty—as you did yesterday—should be able to understand that it was God who did it; that it could not 'just happen.'

I know that you are skeptical about the bible stories. But if you look carefully at that book you might ask yourself how it would be possible for its many authors to have invented those stories, as fairy tales, because they complement each other perfectly and were written over a period of many hundreds of years.

This edition of the bible is called A Study Bible. *There are notations at the bottom of each page that amplify what you've just read. I suggest that you begin with John's gospel, that's the fourth of four, the first four books of the New Testament. It will tell you all you need to know about Jesus Christ. Jesus, as you know, is the One whom I have accepted as my Lord and Savior.*

After you've done that, perhaps we can talk about it.

With much love, Debbie

§

Debbie's note left Roger in an emotional funk. Was she asking him to compete with this mythical Jesus person? How could he possibly do that? On the other hand, what if this Jesus is *not* a mythical person? What if he really is/was who Debbie says he is: *my Lord and Savior?* Then a little voice: *Okay, Roger. This lovely wife of yours is no dummy. Do what she says and read what she's asked you to read. It could make a difference.*

Roger picked up the bible and found what he was looking for: *In the beginning was the Word, and the Word was with God and the Word was God. He was in the beginning with God. All things came into being through Him and apart from Him nothing came into being that has come into being. In Him was life and the life was the Light of men.*

Roger wasn't sure he understood what he had just read. The notes at the bottom of the page helped: 'In the beginning. Before time began,

Christ was already in existence with God. Christ was active in the work of creation.'

'Hmmm, I wonder if that's really possible. And who is this guy, John, the author of this story? Maybe he invented the whole thing. I'll read it all and see if that helps.'

And that's what he did. He read John's gospel, front to back. Some of it was hard to accept. Like feeding those five thousand people or bringing Lazarus back to life after he'd been dead for four days. And how could Jesus suddenly appear in a room when the doors were locked; especially when he was supposed to be dead. It made no sense. But there would be nothing gained by telling Debbie what he thought. He'd keep it to himself and he could tell her, honestly, that he was 'thinking about it.'

Roger 'thought about it' for another two years. He and Debbie, without making an issue of it, worked out a kind of 'truce' which allowed Roger to ask Debbie questions about what he read which, eventually, included the entire New Testament, the Psalms and the book of Proverbs. Roger found himself drawn to Paul's letters and the book of Acts, especially Luke's descriptions of the three missionary journeys. He concluded, somewhat reluctantly, that Luke must have been a first-class historian to have recorded all the details in that book.

Still, he remained skeptical. Christ's crucifixion—that he could understand and the fact that each of the four gospels described it made it believable. But the resurrection—that was something Roger simply couldn't accept.

Twenty Years Later

It was approaching nightfall, but the helicopter pilot had done this many times, landing his Bell-47 squarely in the center of the large, red 'X' painted on the flat rooftop of Colorado Springs' All Saints' Memorial Hospital. Even before the blades stopped spinning, the hospital medics had the gurney in place, ready to offload the injured man. Bob Summerville was first off, shouting above the noise of the rotors that he would explain what had happened as soon as his friend was safely inside. The chopper's pilot had radioed ahead that a Roger Longworth had been injured while on a hunting trip, probably some kind of spinal trauma. He was conscious and not in pain but he was unable to walk, saying his legs were completely numb.

After transferring Roger from the helicopter to the gurney, the medics quickly moved toward the hospital's rooftop entrance, telling Bob that he could find Roger in the hospital's Emergency Room, down at street level. The helicopter pilot had radioed ahead and it was likely that the on-duty ER doctor would be available.

Before the helicopter left its roof-top perch, the pilot asked Bob to sign what he called a 'release ticket,' certifying that the helicopter crew had done its job and that its two passengers had arrived safely. Bob then walked to the elevator, descended to the street-level entrance, and quickly found the Emergency Room.

It was a long wait, as often happens in emergency room settings, but eventually doctor Richard Sherman approached Bob, introduced himself and asked him to come with him to Roger's ER cubicle. He said Roger had blacked out after the accident and couldn't remember what had happened. The doctor hoped that Bob could provide some of the details that would help him with his diagnosis. And, he added,

Roger's wife was on the way. One of the nurses had phoned her as soon as Roger was admitted

§

Bob's story:

The two men had spotted three Big Horn sheep, about a half-mile away, on the far side of a rocky ravine. The wind was blowing toward the hunters so their scent wasn't the problem. But the Big Horn has the best vision of any of the four-footed animals and it was imperative that Bob and Roger not be seen. Bob's plan was to approach the animals from behind and to do that they would descend a steep, talus slope, then climb the far side of the valley, using the larger boulders for cover.

About half-way down the slope, Roger slipped on a piece of loose rock, lost his balance and went tumbling, head first down the slope. He was unable to break his fall which ended when he reached the bottom of the ravine, landing on his back. When Bob reached him, Roger was unconscious but his pulse and breathing were normal. He was bleeding from his scalp, his shirt was torn and his right arm was bleeding at the elbow; one of his boots was missing and there was a large, ugly bruise on his left cheek.

Bob opened his rucksack, pulled out his first aid kit and tried to stop the bleeding. He found two small packages of sulfa powder, sprinkled them into Roger's open wounds and then applied a butterfly bandage to his scalp and elbow. Then he removed the canteen from his belt, soaked his neckerchief and placed it on Roger's forehead. The cold, wet cloth brought Roger around; he opened his eyes and spoke.

"What the hell happened?"

"You took a nasty fall, my friend, and you're pretty well banged up. You'd best lie there while I decide what we do about this."

"That may be a problem, Bob. I don't feel a damned thing from my butt to my toes. No pain, but no feeling, either. I doubt that I can walk out of here. What do you think?"

"I think I'd better see if my Citizens' Band handset can reach someone who can help. I know you don't believe in prayer but something like that would be a good idea."

Bob's years of hiking/hunting and taught him a lesson: Always let the Forest Service know where you're going to be and for how long, something like the flight plans used by civil aviation pilots. And he had written down the CB call sign for the nearest Forest Service office, located about fifteen crow-flight miles from where he thought they were. After several tries, the on-duty Forest Service watch officer responded. She recorded Bob's estimated position and after determining that the two men could not walk to safety she said she'd call for a helicopter.

"So, that's what happened. I know my friend is going to be here for awhile but I'd like to hear what the doctor has to say. Doctor 'Sherman' is it?"

"Yes. It's too early to know for certain, but we'll keep Roger here for a day or two, do the X-rays and run some tests; then we'll develop a plan for his recovery. Surgery may be needed but we just don't know. You can call in to the ER information desk and they'll be able to tell you how our patient is doing."

Before leaving the ER, Debbie walked over to Bob and told him how grateful she was. He had saved her husband's life and for that she would always remember. A true friend, indeed.

§

Three days later, Roger came home, in an ambulance. Debbie had heard from the doctor and after allowing herself a brief crying jag, she prayed that God would lead her to practical decisions. This was a major turning point in her life, something she could not manage on her own. Her answer to that prayer came immediately. She remembered that she was, after all, an RN with years of experience. Doctor Sherman told her that Roger would never walk again. He was permanently paralyzed from the waist down. Everything else about him was perfectly normal. Twenty-twenty eyesight, hand-eye coordination as good as ever, no evidence of brain trauma. Roger would soon learn to get around in a wheel chair and he could resume his teaching regimen at the college as soon as he felt up to it. Debbie would have to make some common-sense adjustments in their home—furniture placements, a ramp into and out of both the front and rear entrances, grab bars in the bathrooms and a motorized stairwell chair between the floors of their two-level rambler.

As Roger was approaching retirement age, he and Debbie decided that life in their lovely home wasn't working out as well as they had hoped. Roger's work at the college was going well enough; he'd been promoted to the head of the college's mathematics department but after a year in that position he decided it was time to move on. There were younger men who could do the job. And mobility was an increasingly-difficult problem for him and it was becoming more and more difficult for Debbie to cope. After discussing it with Roger, she talked to the pastor of her church. She and Roger had already agreed that they should move to some kind of retirement facility, one that could help with Roger's handicap. Her pastor asked her if she had considered a *Christian* community, one that could support Roger's physical requirements and Debbie's spiritual needs.

She told him she'd thought about it but nothing specific had come to mind. The Yellow Pages advertised several such places in the Colorado Springs area but none of those appealed to either her or to Roger. Her pastor asked Debbie if she'd heard about the Colorado Springs Covenant Village, a ten-building campus located west of the metropolitan area, overlooking the United States Air Force Academy. He knew the campus chaplain, he said, and if Debbie and Roger were interested, he'd give her a call. Debbie said she wasn't familiar with that name, *Covenant*.

It's the Evangelical Covenant Church of America. It's a national church with close ties to the Covenant Retirement Communities organization. CRC has twelve campuses in the United States, one of them right here in Colorado Springs. Like your own church, Debbie, it's a Christ-centered, loving and diverse community that welcomes anyone over the age of fifty-five. You don't even have to be a believer to live there, although nearly everyone is. And, from what you've shared with me about your husband's agnosticism, I'm sure he'd feel very comfortable in that environment.

Debbie agreed to meet the village chaplain, Jennifer Yarborough. The appointment was set for the following morning and Roger, in his wheel-chair and in their specially-modified van, would come with her.

§

Jennifer Yarborough had been in the Covenant Church family for more than forty years and this was her fifth year as the Covenant Village chaplain. She met the Longworth's van at the village entrance and es-corted them to her office. It was obvious to Roger that the woman knew how to respond to someone confined to a wheel chair and that was all he needed to know. Debbie felt the same way; this was a woman they could trust and who could help. 'Chaplain Jenny' was the way she wanted to be addressed and after the introductions she gave the Longworths a 'spoken tour' of the village: its residency requirements, costs of services, on-campus facilities, including a therapy department that Roger would find helpful.

Following the briefing, as Roger and Debbie were about to leave, Chaplain Jenny handed Debbie a brochure that explained the on-campus BeFriender ministry. She knew that Roger was a self-proclaimed agnostic, that this had been a source of tension in the marriage for many years and that Debbie might find some helpful ideas. But that would be later. For now, the Longworths would have to wait until an apartment became available.

§

Roger couldn't have been more surprised, and pleased. He and Debbie were having dinner in the village dining room, their third such since moving to the village a week earlier. Seated at the same table was Jeffery Atkins, a sixty-something retired high school football and basketball coach and a 'sports fanatic' as he referred to himself. He said he'd been following the University of Washington's rowing program for many years and because there was nothing of the kind in the state of Colorado he had adopted the Huskies as his own favorite crew.

Over dinner, Atkins told Roger about his career as a high school coach, how he'd watched his students grow to mature men and women, some of whom were still writing him letters. One of them, sad to say, had been injured in a automobile accident and was now confined to a wheel chair, much like Roger. And what happened to Roger? Why the wheel chair? A hunting mishap? Jeffery could relate to that. He'd been hunting many times in the Colorado mountains, Wyoming's too. He had yet to bag a mountain goat, although he'd come close two years ago while hunting on Colorado's Mount Massive.

Debbie understood that this dinner encounter had been arranged the day before by Chaplain Jenny. Jeffery Atkins was part of the village BeFriender team and Jenny believed the two men would like each other, owing to their mutual interests. And she was right. They became *very* good friends, with Jeff Atkins making sure that he spent some time with Roger at least once each week.

During their fourth visit Jeff told Roger about his long-time membership in the Faith Covenant Church, the church that was an unofficial sponsor of the Colorado Springs Covenant Village. Would Roger like to come with him next Sunday? Well, maybe. He knew it would please his wife and, who knows, he might even get used to the idea.

Following the church service, Roger asked Jeff to meet him in the church library. He had something on his mind and he wanted to talk about it, privately.

Did Jeff believe it possible that a life-long agnostic could become a Christian believer? What would it take? Roger confessed that his marriage to Debbie could have been so much more meaningful, especially to her, if only he had been a believer from the get-go.

Jeff's response was direct enough. He said, 'Look, Roger. I'm not here to give you advice. I can only talk about what I know to be true and you can take it or leave it.

'There are about five hundred people living in our Covenant Village. Ninety-five percent of them are believers, committed Christians. In the Colorado Springs metropolitan area there are some forty to fifty thousand church-goers, all denominations. Do you think it likely that all of these people are *wrong*? You've read the bible, a lot of it. What is it about those readings that you *don't* believe? And what is the number of Christians, world-wide? Close to *two billion*, at last count. Do you think all of those people are *wrong*? And everyone of us reads the same bible, the same scriptures, the Word of God. And how is that possible? It's because the bible has been translated into more than five hundred languages. Can you think of another book that can claim that number?

'You're a smart guy, my friend. You're closer than you think to joining your wife, and me, and a whole bunch of others.'

§

Jeffery Atkins, the Covenant Village BeFriender, was *almost* right. Roger was still skeptical but with Debbie's and Jeff Atkins' continuing encouragement, and many prayers, they were satisfied that, eventually, Roger Longworth would accept Jesus as his Lord and Savior.

CHAPTER 10
Mary

§

Author's note: This is a story that was brought to my attention by a BeFriender, a resident of the Bellevue (Nebraska) Covenant Village. It is a striking example of a deep and abiding friendship that developed between the BeFriender and the one befriended. It appears here with her permission.

§

Mary (not her real name) was born on a farm in the west-central part of Nebraska, not far from the North Platte River. Most of us are old enough to remember, even as children, what farming was like in this state during the Great Depression. It was tough, especially during those sub-zero winters. Mary's parents had a lease on 160 acres of wheat and barley and another twenty acres for the hay they needed to feed their animals. The property came with a small barn for their five milk cows and a couple of chicken coops. And they also raised pigs, for the bacon and ham. So, like most farmers of that era, they tried to be self-sufficient.

Mary was three years older than her baby sister, Alice, and her mother expected her to look after her as soon as she was old enough. She told me that if she'd had just one brother, her life as a child would have been a little easier. To understand what she meant by that you need to know that her father died when she had just turned thirteen. That meant that her mother had to find someone to help run the farm, which she did by hiring a twenty-two-year-old who had grown up in Omaha. Tom Bradshaw knew enough about farming to help and that arrangement worked well for the first six months or so. But then, late one afternoon when he'd finished his chores, he tried to molest Mary. She fought him off, ran into the house screaming and told her mother what had happened. After Mary had calmed down her mother explained to her that it wouldn't do any good to tell the police because it would be her word against Tom's. Tom never set foot on that farm again, knowing that if he did he'd have to talk to the county sheriff. Of course little Alice had a pretty good idea about what had happened and from that day forward she looked up to Mary as if she were some kind of saint.

Mary told me that that one experience with Tom changed her entire outlook on life and especially about men. At age thirteen, she had already begun to mature and she realized that she had come very close to being raped. And if that weren't bad enough she had persuaded herself that she had to hide this awful experience. No one to talk to except, of course, her mother.

And there's another part of this story that's important. Mary, her mother and sister Alice had been going to the local Four Square Gospel Mission church. Her mother taught Sunday School in that church and Mary and Alice were baptized there. The church's pastor was a sixty-year-old man, and a genuine saint. Everyone in the congregation loved him and it really hurt Mary to know that she could never tell Pastor Stephen about her experience with Tom. And the more she thought about it, the more she wondered about what she was reading in her bible. Why did God allow Tom to come into her life? And how could her nearly being raped fit with what Apostle Paul wrote that 'all things work together for good?' She didn't understand; she couldn't ask her pastor for help and her mother didn't have answers. Mary told me that her faith had been so shaken by these events that she thought about killing herself. She had prayed about this and God's answer, she believed, was to *Wait a little longer, My child, help is on the way.*

That *help* arrived in a way she could never have imagined. One of Mary's Sunday School friends was a girl her age, Vicky Johnson. Vicky told her that she had been aware that Tom was working on Mary's farm. Vicky knew that Tom had tried to rape her older sister but she was able to get away by screaming for help. Then she waited a day to report the event to the local police. The police couldn't do anything about it because there were no witnesses, another of those 'he-said-she-said' situations. Then Vicky asked Mary, point-blank, 'Did Tom ever try to do anything like that to *you?*' And that was what she had been waiting to hear, someone who was really concerned about her. After her sobbing had stopped, Mary told Vicky the whole story.

That experience, with Vicky, stayed in Mary's memory until her dying day. It was a new friendship, rooted in love and trust. Although each of them was only thirteen years old, when she thought back on it Mary believed it to be the most memorable event of her life. The two girls quickly became 'best buddies' and began going to church together. That church had a small singing group and its leader taught the youngsters a few of those old-time gospel melodies. Mary's favorites were *How Awesome is Our God* and *I Will Trust.*

$$\text{\S}$$

We can move along now to the time when Mary had finished high school. She had to part ways with her best buddy because Vicky's parents had lost their farm. You may remember that bitter winter of 1952, when the temperatures stayed near zero for nearly a month; it killed all their livestock and that meant they couldn't make the mortgage payments. So they had no choice and they moved to California to be closer to their relatives.

That was another heartache for Mary, to say good-bye to her best friend. They wrote letters to each other but it wasn't the same; and long distance telephone calls were too expensive.

Before learning that Vicky was leaving, Mary enrolled in a nurses' training program at one of Omaha's community colleges. A good thing, too, because her course work kept her so busy she had little time to think about how much she missed Vicky. She finished that program in three years and after taking the tests required by Nebraska state law, she was licensed as a Registered Nurse.

You might think there could have been some men her life as she went through those three years of training. Well, there was, just one. His name was Dan Henning and, like Mary, he'd decided to devote his life to helping other people. His plan was to begin as a male nurse and then, as opportunities came along, he would move up. Dan was able to help Mary forget about Tom and after dating for about a year they decided to get married.

When Mary told me what happened next, she said she was convinced that Satan had jumped back into her life, as though he wanted to replace Tom with something else. It seems that while Dan was helping one of the doctors in the hospital's emergency room, he picked up an infection that quickly morphed into a strain of blood poisoning for which there was no known cure. The poor man died within a month—with Mary at his bedside, holding his hand.

Mary was so distressed over Dan's passing that she entered a counseling program, right there in the hospital. She met mostly with the hospital's chaplain and, eventually, she decided she could function again, more or less as she had before. But, as she told me later, she was a changed person. She had decided she'd rather grow up as an old maid, than to risk another heartache. And she stuck to her word. She never did marry.

§

If nothing else, Mary was smart. After getting her RN certificate she went to work for Saint Mary's Hospital in downtown Omaha. This was long before Medicare and to make ends meet the hospital had to rely on donations from churches and a few wealthy Christians. The job didn't pay much but she loved her work and it wasn't long before she was one of the favorites, especially among the physicians and surgeons. I've wondered about that, how this woman with those huge disappointments in her life could manage such a cheerful disposition.

But she did manage and after four years in that same hospital she was promoted to head nurse in the OB/GYN department. She probably thought that if she wasn't going to have children of her own, at least she could hold and love the infant children of other parents.

Mary stayed with that job for another twenty years and by that time she was virtually running the hospital. She knew every doctor by name, every nurse, even the janitors and ambulance drivers. She even tried to memorize the names of each patient by reading the admittance slips as they came across her desk. At one time the hospital's manager asked her if she'd like to come aboard as his assistant. She begged off, claiming she knew nothing about 'administration,' and preferred to do what she was doing.

§

At age sixty-five, Mary decided it was time to retire. She had been wise with her money and the hospital had a decent pension fund in which she was well invested. She didn't want to stay in the same, small apartment that had been her home for all those years; she wanted something different. Where to begin looking? Then she remembered the hospital's chaplain, a man with a church background that Mary didn't know much about: The Evangelical Covenant Church of America.

During her visit with the chaplain, he told her about our Bellevue Covenant Village, explained how one applies, the various kinds of services that are offered. He told her that if she were interested he could place a call to the village's marketing director, broker an introduction and Mary could do the rest. And, sure enough, some time later Mary became a new resident. She made new friends quickly, came to Sunday worship every week and began to enjoy the next phase of her life.

But then, more bad news. She received a telephone call from the same hospital in which she had worked, saying that her sister Alice had just been admitted, having suffered a stroke the previous evening. She wasn't expected to live through the day and could Mary come to visit her, *now*. Of course, Mary left the village immediately but found the traffic so heavy that by the time she reached the hospital Alice had already died. And Mary, as the sole survivor in what was left of the family, had to plan the funeral. You can see where this is going: This is one very depressed and lonely woman, or that's the way she thought of herself.

The funeral was a quiet affair, held in Omaha's Church of the Nazarene. Several of Mary's village friends went with her, knowing she needed the moral support. After the graveside service, one of Mary's friends brought her back to the village and after thanking everyone, she walked into her apartment, locked the door and we didn't see her again for nearly a week. By that time I knew her well enough to telephone her, to ask if there was anything I could do to help. Her response surprised me in a way, although maybe it shouldn't have. She said she was fine, she had plenty of food in the fridge and she just wanted some quiet time to be by herself, to think about all the good times she and Alice had had together, to pray and to read her bible.

You all know me well enough by now: I'm certainly not a psychiatrist but I could tell that Mary had fallen into a deep depression; and who could blame her? Alice had been Mary's only living relative and now she was all by herself. And it was at that point that I decided to bring all this to the attention of chaplain Marsha. Marsha knows the rest of the story but she has asked me to finish it.

When Mary decided to come out of her seclusion, she called me and asked if we could have lunch together. Well, I jumped at the opportunity and over lunch—and I had discussed this with Marsha a few days earlier—I told Mary about our BeFriender program. I explained to her how I had been in the program for some time and that if she thought it would help I would be more than happy to visit with her and listen to whatever she had to say. I also assured her that whatever we talked about would go no further, that we were quite serious about confidentiality. And I promised her that she could say, or not say, anything she wished; it was up to her. But, she might find that a sympathetic ear, belonging to a friend she could trust, could be quite comforting.

Mary asked me to give her some time to think about it and the next day she said she'd like to have me come to her apartment for our first visit. I did that and those visits continued, once each week, for the next six months. Mary told me everything I've just told you and some other things, as well. What she did *not* tell me—and I learned this only a few days ago—she had been dealing with pancreatic cancer and it was too late for treatment. She told the head nurse about this but no one else.

As I think you already know, Mary passed away just last week. She had been heavily sedated and, I am told, she didn't suffer. What else can I say, except that it was a real privilege to be her friend.

About the Author

JOHN SAGER IS A RETIRED United States Intelligence Officer whose services for the CIA, in various capacities, spanned more than fifty years. A widower, he makes his home in the Covenant Shores retirement community on Mercer Island, Washington.

Made in the USA
Coppell, TX
03 April 2020